To
David

AWAKEN Your
Dreams

Live Your Possibilites
You're A Great Man.
Thanks for all You
Do..!! DYOF

A Slap On The Back Of The Head

Acts of Love, Life Lessons and a Journey to Success

By Giulio Veglio

Foreword by John Paul DeJoria
and Winn Claybaugh

Praise for
A Slap On The Back Of The Head

"This is a candid, inspiring, heartwarming and courageous book packed with life lessons and terrific insights about what it takes to be truly successful in business and in life. This is a must read for anyone who wants to increase the chances for success and happiness NOW."

— Charles Marcus, business savvy motivational speaker and
best-selling author of *Success is Not a Spectator Sport*

"*A Slap on the Back of the Head* is a true 'reality book.' Giulio Veglio shares his personal life, both good and bad, and reveals how he overcame obstacles that we all face in different forms. He learned the importance of being mentored and then giving back. Success always comes to those who are willing to help others be successful. Giulio is a testimony to that."

— John M. McCormack, founder and CEO, Visible Changes,
and best-selling author of *Self-Made in America*

"This is a masterfully written true story that will take you on a journey to capture your heart and imagination."

— Dennis and Gary Ratner, Ratner Companies

"Giulio's life journey is fun to read, yet serious when it needs to be. The lessons are many and wise. It offers a wonderful experience for everyone who reads it, especially those that grew up in an Italian home. Thank you, Giulio, for sharing your story, and please say 'hi' to Sonny and Vin."

— Luke Jacobellis, president, John Paul Mitchell Systems

"There is a common thread in the book that every immigrant to this country can relate to — I did! Giulio offers the quintessential American success story that, when read and applied, will inspire and help others on their journey."

— James Morrison, cofounder and co-owner, Toni&Guy

"Giulio Veglio has written down his soul in his new book. His voice is vibrant, loud, funny and crystal clear. Reading about his journey has been nothing but a pleasure!"

— Joan Harrison, publisher, Harco Publishing

"Life has its lessons, and when people are humble enough to share their story, it changes the world's energy. Now I can truly appreciate what has shaped Giulio's ability to grow and achieve personal greatness. I thank him for his honesty and, most importantly, for helping change so many lives."

> — Stephanie Kocielski, artistic director,
> John Paul Mitchell Systems

"My wife wants to know why the light is still on and I'm still awake. I told her, someone keeps slapping me on the back of my head! This is a good sign. Good night and good reading."

> — Sam Brocato, beauty entrepreneur and master stylist

"Working for Giulio 14 years ago, I only saw him as a man whose life was full and complete. After reading this book, I learned things about my mentor that I never even knew. I am so happy that he can finally see himself the way he is perceived by others because he is truly one in a million!"

> — Mary Cuomo, international platform artist

"I've seen and been around Giulio for years and never knew his full story. From watching him on stage at seminars to now reading his book, I finally understand Giulio's journey — and the value he has in each of the lives he gets to touch every day, including my own!"

> — Robert Cromeans, businessman, salon owner and artistic
> director for John Paul Mitchell Systems

"I read it in one day! It's a good story that inspires."

> — Toni Juskey, teacher

"This is one of those books that when you have it in your hands, you can't put it down. It is a story that is full of the simple truths in life that we so often ignore. It offers a powerful perspective."

> — Ana Slamic, hairstylist and manager of over 100 salons
> in Slovenia

"Whether you are 16 or 61, *A Slap on the Back of the Head* shows there is always a way to start over — even when hitting rock bottom. It encourages me to make my life even better."

> — Lexie Torres, 16-year-old high school student

A Slap on the Back of the Head

Published by Visionary Freak Media,
An imprint of Visionary Freak LLC
800 Spring Valley Road
Altamonte Springs, Florida 32714
866-998-4226

Content Management and Editorial Development: Merry Bateman
Art Direction: Camille Saad
Design: Esther Mejia

Printed in China
10 9 8 7 6 5 4 3 2 1

ISBN: 0-9842604-0-9

Visit us on the web!
www.visionaryfreak.com

THIS IS DEDICATED TO MY PARENTS
WHO SHOWED ME THE WAY.

THEY LOVED THE LIFE THEY LIVED
AND LIVED THE LIFE THEY LOVED!

Contents

Part Four: Change Is A State Of Mind

Foreword
Two Perspectives On Giulio

When I met Giulio Veglio for the first time, there was one thing that stood out about him above anything else: his great sense of humor. Now some 20 years later, I continue to admire his exceptional way of finding humor within himself as well as his wonderful ability to share it with others.

Another side of Giulio that I appreciate is his high regard for family. He is one of the most caring family men that I know. Considering the loving parents and extended family that gave him such strong values, it's no wonder that he has developed this remarkable attitude. As you read this book, it is abundantly clear why family is so important to Giulio and shapes everything he does.

Giulio is a very unique individual and his book reflects his unique journey in life. The book conveys an interesting story about a special man. But it also offers important lessons for us all to reflect upon about our own lives.

I am sure you will find this book as delightful and distinctive as the author, a person I am proud to call a colleague and friend.

John Paul DeJoria
Chairman and CEO, John Paul Mitchell Systems

The first person who came along in my early career was Giulio Veglio. We met at an educational event in 1989, where I was presenting the business side of the beauty industry and he represented the artistic side. I was brand new in my career and scared to death. Would the audience like me? Would they believe me? Lucky for me, Giulio was there. We immediately connected and instantly knew that we would somehow be linked for life. Before long, we were scheming on ways to work with each other and booking ourselves at the same events, turning our business travel into mini-playtime vacations as well.

Over the years, our friendship and eventual business partnership taught me that I could be selfish with whom I decide to do business. Working with Giulio is always fun and always an adventure. I have never questioned his loyalty and love, and he's definitely someone I not only want to work and play with but also someone I can confide in with total comfort and security.

I've learned through past mistakes that if I were to whine and complain to friends or business associates, they might jump to all sorts of inaccurate conclusions. For that reason, my friends, co-workers and I use and practice a system we call "Who's Your Bitch-Buddy?" A bitch-buddy is someone you can gripe to — a nonjudgmental, confidential sounding board, a person you can talk to when you feel bitter, mean, nasty, and ugly.

Giulio has been my best friend and bitch-buddy for many, many years. He's the one person I go to when I need a listening, nonjudgmental ear as I download my latest thoughts, adventures and struggles, and I do the same for him. The safety we feel in our relationship has let us switch those roles back and forth, over and over and over again, many times in the past 20 years. Neither of us has a monopoly on giving or taking advice.

In the past 20 years, Giulio and I have become partners in multiple businesses, shared the stage in front of thousands of people, vacationed with each other all over the world, invited each other's families into our homes countless times, and been there for each other through marriages, deaths, family celebrations, overcoming addictions, and everything else that's occurred in our lives. I often say that I feel sorry for anyone who is not us.

When it comes to my relationship with Giulio, the respect that I have for him, and how much I love this man, I feel sorry for anyone who is not friends with Giulio Veglio. At Paul Mitchell Schools, one of our mission statements is: "When people come first, success will follow." I think I can safely say that no one who knows Giulio has ever felt like he didn't put them first.

As a businessman, Giulio knows how to attract the right people, how to set up a successful business model, and how to make money. Of course, those characteristics describe many other people, too. What sets Giulio apart is that he does all of it with his gifts and talents of humor and making things fun. I'm the type of person who needs to have fun, especially when it comes to work, and I have a feeling that most people are like me.

Although Giulio's humor and talent for making things fun could fool people into thinking he's not a brilliant businessman, he can laugh all the way to the bank with that misperception. Giulio is brilliant — plain and simple — and so is his beautiful book.

Winn Claybaugh
Dean and Cofounder, Paul Mitchell Schools

Introduction

In the beginning, God created the oyster. He said, "Oyster, I'm going to give you the most perfect living environment you could ever imagine." He gave the oyster shelter in the form of a hard shell. He gave the oyster food. Just by opening his mouth food rushes in. He gave the oyster protection by placing him at the bottom of the ocean away from his predators. God gave the oyster everything he needs to survive, but the oyster will never go far.

Then God created the eagle. He said, "Go ahead eagle. Pick a place for a house, but you'll have to build it yourself. There's food out there, but you'll have to go find it yourself. There is not protection for you, other than the gift of flight I have given you, so you will have to do this yourself. You must create your existence, and you can go anywhere you want."

The oyster gets everything he needs, but he won't ever go far. Eagles live risky lives in treetops working hard to survive, but their boundaries are limitless.

When I heard this story for the first time in 2002, I was at the opening of a new Paul Mitchell School. As I listened to John Paul DeJoria, CEO of John Paul Mitchell Systems describe the fable of the oyster and the eagle, I experienced a magical "light bulb" moment. I owe him a debt of gratitude for telling this tale when he did because that's the instant I realized exactly how I could make a difference. This story is one that John Paul has told frequently over the years because he is so passionate about what it conveys to our profession as we strive to be the best we can.

From that point, I made it my personal mission to inspire and encourage people to understand that they can overcome their struggles and challenges in life. I set the intention to influence those that I would come in contact with so that they might accomplish three things: to soar like an eagle, to shape their own existence and to know no boundaries!

When I see an opening to help an individual understand his or her value, or even to lend support in a tough situation, I take that opportunity. I see each of those opportunities as a gift. It's there for me to unwrap to find a rewarding challenge inside.

I fly all over the world with my work. Since I'm a pretty friendly guy, I meet lots of people in airports, on planes and on the ground in new places. They come from all walks of life with different jobs, different lifestyles and different goals. There is one thing that I have confirmed over and over. No matter what part of the world, everyone has struggled with self-confidence at one time or another. And many still do.

It's funny that someone like me, who barely made it through school himself, now owns ten Paul Mitchell Schools plus a fantastic new salon franchise called Lunatic Fringe. I am in a wonderful position to encourage lots of people.

What's cool about what we do through the schools is to design our programs around the concept that everyone learns differently. I wish they had done this in elementary school for me!

School was always a HUGE challenge for me. I remember one day when I was 6 years old, hunched over my desk, struggling to write even the simplest of words. I was fidgety, tugging at my neatly pressed collar. My mother had always made sure I looked spiffy for school, hair slicked down, shirt tucked in.

I distractedly traced over some letters scratched into the worn wooden desk, since I wasn't doing the assignment the teacher was waiting for us to finish. I kept my head low, so maybe the teacher wouldn't notice that, once again, I wasn't joining the class in completing the paper. I tried to make myself as tiny as possible as I saw that one by one, my classmates were putting their pencils down and looking around the classroom. "It's all done now except for the yelling," I thought to myself. I knew that was next; it always was.

Since coming to America from Italy a few months earlier, I hadn't learned much English, so I couldn't understand what the teacher was saying. I always tried, and as the days went by, I did pick up some of the frequent words I heard around me including "stupid," "idiot" and "dumb."

Even now, all these years later, as I write these words, I remember how rotten that felt. I remember how the teacher made me feel. And I remember how frustrated I was at my inability to understand what was going on.

That frustration and hurt haunted me all the way through grade school, high school, hair styling school and beyond. It really did a number on me! I constantly see how our own minds work against us. We know the truth but we bury it under all the layers of self-doubt, self-loathing and self-mistrust.

Although those times seemed horrible for me when they occurred, they made me stronger. I believe I went through what I did so I could help others see that they're not alone. I decided to write this book to document my experience of going from feeling worthless to becoming someone.

This is the story of my journey to finding my truth, and who I listened to along that journey, the influences I allowed to impact my decisions and my life. I overcame a lack of belief in myself, drug addiction, even a coma that was followed by a lengthy recovery. I didn't know what my truth was until I got to the other end of it. I'm hoping to help others find their truth and enjoy success like I have.

And I have enjoyed success! For one thing, I have a successful marriage. Hey, any marriage that lasts 20 years or more in this day and age is pretty successful, right? Love my Laura. And I have two beautiful, smart, good boys that bless me every day. I did something right!

I feel so fortunate to have been able to find my self-confidence; to realize that I had to love myself before I could do anything else. Whether someone is trying to quit drugs, lose weight, start a business, or just get through life, they have to discover the love for themselves first. That is the key to success. That IS success!

If, by reading this book, just one person can feel a little bit better about himself; if just one person can know that she is not alone in feeling stupid; if just one person can make a better choice for his life; if just one person can find a way out of her oyster shell to venture forth; then I have succeeded in my purpose for writing.

To each and everyone, may you have belief in yourself to soar like an eagle!

Giulio Veglio
Casselberry, Florida
Summer, 2009

Part One

It Begins

La Dolce Vita

1.
Italia

Kneeling on the plush sofa with my arms folded over the back, I was anxiously looking out the window waiting for my dad to come home. In the kitchen, my mother bustled about, doing what she loved by preparing a delicious dinner for us. My sisters, Maria and Elvira, were squabbling about something I didn't care about and Giuseppe, my brother, was nowhere to be found.

I peered down the street as far around the bushes out front as I could, like I did every night. I loved the way he walked down the street. He always dressed "to the nines," wearing his fedora jauntily pulled down, so it was almost over his left eye.

I had heard my grandmother say that my dad was our village's biggest flirt before he met my mother. She called him a real "ladies man." But after meeting the beautiful woman who would become my mother, he only had eyes for her.

We lived *la dolce vita*, the sweet life. My mother had everything she wanted — glamorous clothes, jewelry and luxurious living. That wasn't bad for someone with only a fifth grade education. Don't get me wrong. My mother was smarter than most people far more educated than she. She was always very connected with everyone she encountered because of an uncanny intuitive ability to read people. She understood their motives.

Growing up, my mother lived on a dairy farm. Her mother was a schoolteacher, but they really didn't see the need to educate her beyond fifth grade. My mother would take horse and carriage and go into Naples to sell the cheese that her father made on the farm. Her other six siblings always wondered how she sold so much cheese — she was always the first one home with an empty carriage.

Customers tried to take advantage of her. They would see the petite, vivacious young beauty and try to rip her off, but she would have none of it.

"Vattene! Vattene," she would say, shaking her fist at them. Her high cheekbones flushed with anger as she commanded: "Get out of here!"

Yes, she had common sense that comes with street smarts. And she had my dad. *"Lui è stato il mio primo amore,"* she always said. "He was my first love, you know."

People were always bringing gifts to our house, although my father never accepted bribes, as he was a man of great integrity. He had a good government job. As the chief tax collector for our village, he was also in charge of the whole division for the state.

Everyone knew who he was and his position was respected. When we walked down the street, both women and men would go out of their way to greet my handsome papa. It was agreed that he was *un bell'uomo*. But good looks aside, my father was also very powerful in our village.

It was 1967 in Alvignano, in the province of Caserta, which is about 28 miles north of Naples, Italy. Our country was still in a state of reconstruction after we had been defeated in World War II. It was a long road to recovery that we were traveling, and the aftermath was being felt in many ways. If someone wanted to build something, they had to get their request approved through my father. If they wanted to sell something, he was the one to authorize it. If they failed to report their actions, my papa was the one who put them in jail.

Even at the tender age of 5, I guessed that sometimes his job could be dangerous, since he always carried a gun in his belt. I spent many an afternoon imagining him using his pistol to ward off bad guys. That just added to my adoration of my father. He was *ammaliante*, so fascinating to me.

The squeak of the front gate jolted me from my reverie, and I realized that he was home.

"*Babbo, Babbo,*" I yelled, running to greet him at the door.

Being the baby of the family, I felt that this was my job — to make sure papa got home each night. He looked down at me as he came through the door, and smoothly removed his hat and gave me a kiss and a slap on the back of the head at the same time. It was his way of saying "I love you," and I loved him for it.

Usually after dinner was playtime with dad, but the last few nights had been different. He and mama had been having animated conversations that continued long after we were tucked into bed.

As my brother and sisters and I played in the next room, we heard the word "America" spoken often. We weren't exactly sure what "America" was, but in our vivid imaginations, it was a land with candy everywhere and theme park rides on every street corner.

It seemed like a sharp contrast to our beloved Italia. Of course we loved our home, our village, our family, our friends and neighbors. But many of them were feeling as desperate as the landscape still looked. The damage that was done during the war went far beyond what the eye could see. It also caused a loss of many jobs in Italy. Even many of the most highly educated people were without work.

My father was one of the lucky ones. He not only had a job, but it was a good one in the government. Due to his prestigious position, friends and neighbors regularly approached him for help finding work. He was distressed about what the future held for his children, and had heard that America was the "land of opportunity."

In addition, the Refugee Relief Act of 1953 made it seem possible that even Italians would be welcomed in America. This was enticing to many, and thousands of Italians immigrated after the war. But, America was rumored to have been overwhelmed by the influx of immigrants, and they began to place limits on the number of visas that would be granted.

In 1965, amendments to the Immigration and Nationality Act abolished the nation-origin quotas and established an annual limitation of 170,000 visas for immigrants.

In 1968, the United States would decide to limit the number of visas to 120,000, and it was on a first come, first serve basis. Perhaps my father had heard about it in advance, and that is why the decision was made to make the move to America, and fast.

Our parents wanted life to be better for us than what it was for their friends in Italy. They had a *fantastica* life, but knew the chances for us to have a life even remotely like theirs was next to impossible if they remained in Italy. They were convinced that the opportunities were not available in Italy like they would be for us in America.

They loved us in a way that made them pack everything up, pull together all their money and move. In their heads were visions of affording us better educations, deeper pockets of opportunity, and a variety of unbelievable possibilities. This drastic uprooting was an act of total sacrifice for their children.

For us, my parents were willing to give up their personal wealth, prestigious lifestyle and respected position. It has impressed me my whole life to think how they gave up everything for us. At the time, I don't know if anyone really knew just how much they were giving up.

Family always comes first.

2.
Bon Voyage

And so the decision was made, we would move to America. Mama and Maria would accompany our household goods on a ship, while papa, Elvira, Giuseppe and I flew over so papa could start working. We had relatives in America who were going to help us get settled.

"Why is everybody crying?" I asked myself.

It seemed like the entire town came to the airport to say goodbye to the families that were going to America. Everyone was hugging and tears flowed like a river. I kind of stayed off to myself, hanging out with a few other boys who were in the same situation. We were too wound up to cry.

All of our families navigated our way to the gate, each of us kids holding tight to the toys our families had bought us to keep us occupied on the long flight. My papa had bought me a toy gun.

We tried to be good on the flight. We really did. It all started when papa took me to the restroom. With the cramped quarters that those airplane potties offered, he decided to return to his seat, since I, uh, well, I was gonna be a while, you know?

So, when I was done, I called for my papa. Then, when he didn't come, I did what any 5-year-old who still needed a bit of help at times would do. I went to find him with my pants around my ankles. Well? I needed help! What was I supposed to do?

The giggles and snorts of the other passengers as I made my way down the aisle alerted him to my procession. He turned around just as I approached his seat and the horrified look on his face was the first time I considered that I probably should have thought twice before wandering around the plane with my pants down.

He wasn't as mad as he was embarrassed, but my papa was a little harsh on the cleanup, if you know what I mean. But he was not nearly as harsh as he was going to be. I just couldn't seem to stay out of trouble on that flight.

I tried, really. But it was just so BORING! I sat in my seat, squirming and restless. I began to consider ways to entertain myself. I asked myself: "How could I make the stewardess jump?" Just as I was thinking how much fun this would be to do with one of my friends back home, a boy I knew appeared. His name was Sonny and he always seemed to show up when I was about to do something I shouldn't!

Soon, Sonny and I were conspiring to make the stewardess jump. We were pretty sure she would think it was funny. I clutched the toy pistol to my chest as Sonny and I crouched behind the cover of a navy blue airplane seat. We were hiding in ambush.

"Wait for her to come down the aisle," Sonny whispered to me as he adjusted his position behind me to get a better look around the seat.

I began to feel the burn in my legs as I crouched behind the seat, but he had a plan and I wasn't going to move. We tracked the progress of the stewardess in our direction by listening and taking quick peeks. Slowly but surely she filled drink orders closer and closer to our position. Her hands moved efficiently and she made her way closer.

"Almost...almost...NOW," Sonny whispered as he pushed me ahead of him into the aisle. Like shooting darts we screamed.

"BANG! Bang. BANG!"

The stewardess' frozen smile became a grimace as she jumped and struggled to contain her tray of drinks. Drinks spilled everywhere randomly showering several seats and passengers. A chorus of curses flew, a flurry of napkins followed in attempts to dab up the soda and juices dripping from seats and people.

"*Che figata!*" Cool! Feeling the toy gun in my hand, the power of the moment made me grin like a fool. It was great.

Sonny doubled over next to me, absorbed in a full-grown giggle fest. The stewardess was not amused. Her lips pursed together and an angry flush spread across her cheeks.

And as the thrill — the triumphant adrenaline pumped through us — a stern man got up from his seat and placed an earnest deadlock on my eyes. He was on a deliberate mission to stop the boys and punish them for their deeds. He scooped us both up by the collar and painfully escorted us back up the aisle. He roughly arranged us back into our seats with the other families.

Sonny and I were silenced by the sternness in his expression and the power of being placed so directly into our seats. Another boy I knew, Vin, was sitting next to the window and busying himself by drawing on some napkins.

My father's right hand was making a *"What the f---are you doing?!"* gesture just inches from my nose. You know, the one really pissed off Italians always make where the two fingers are put together with the thumb and wave, in front of the face, a la "thatsa spicy meataballa!" Only that's not what it means.

The fingers on his left hand lifted my face to his by pulling the tender skin under my chin upward. Ouch! It hurt like hell. Tears stung the backs of my eyelids as I squirmed in my father's grasp.

"It isn't fair," I thought to myself. I was just having fun. As my skin screamed under my father's powerful fingers, Vin began shrinking down, trying to become invisible. When the scolding was finished I was left with a throbbing jaw and the memory of my father's disappointed expression. He wanted me to grow up strong and proper. I wasn't doing too well on that front. He seemed embarrassed. Again.

Well, of course he was. I was really a bugger on the whole flight. Can you imagine if a kid had a toy gun on a flight today? Especially with what I did, I would've had the air marshall all over me and probably been in handcuffs, too!

Sonny and I would remain locked down for the remainder of the flight. My father made sure of that by sitting directly behind us. After what seemed like an hour, Vin looked up from the napkin that he was quietly drawing on and looked me up and down.

Leaning over he asked, "What were you doing?" He made that well-known Italian gesture. It was certainly as well-known to me then as it is today.

"Nothing. We were just playing with my gun," I replied.

"Yeah, well you sure made your dad angry," Vin said as he looked down at his drawings.

Then he looked back at me and asked, "Are you happy? Do you like getting into trouble with Sonny?" The words came out slow and cautious.

"I don't know," I shrugged. What? I didn't mean it. It was an accident. Why does everyone hate me? It's not my fault she spilled the drinks. I was just playing. Why are they blaming me? I didn't know the drinks would spill. How could I know? I was just trying to be funny — to make people laugh. I was always trying to get people to laugh. Folding my arms, I pushed my small body back in the seat. I closed my eyes and looked as if I was trying to sleep. I decided to take Vin's lead and try to disappear.

Now, dear reader, hit the pause button a moment. I am going to quickly detour from this story for your benefit. You should know that Sonny and Vin are my best friends while being imaginary. They are always around me. And they seem very real to me, especially when I am in turmoil of some sort, or about to get in trouble.

Vin, the peacemaker, appears older and wiser than Sonny. He is filled with logic and sensibility as well as intuitive foresight. He can see a train wreck 20 miles down the track and he avoids it.

Sonny, dear Sonny, is my saboteur. Sonny is the one who makes it hard to succeed, hard to get out of bed in the morning, hard to pull away from addiction.

You'll find Sonny and Vin around so much because they are my alter egos. They are the subconscious voices that influence me in almost everything I do.

I tell you this for clarity before I go deeper into the twists and turns that my journey takes.

With that in mind, let's get back to the story where I was feigning sleep on the plane.

By now I could feel the plane easing down as it began to make its descent into the New York area. We scrunched up against papa trying to peer out the window to see our new home. Excitement charged through us all. I took turns scrambling over Vin and papa and whoever else we could find by a window. As we flew into New York, we saw this huge statue of a lady in the water, holding fire in her hand, like a torch! We thought it was the funniest thing we had ever seen!

The adults on the plane were as excited as the children were, of course. The stewardesses had a heck of a time trying to get the passengers in seats in order to land. We were sequestered to our seats for the rest of the flight. Not to be held down, Sonny and I bounced up and down in our seats trying to help the plane land faster.

Once we hit the ground I shouted excitedly, *"Siamo qui! Siamo qui! Siamo arrivati nell'America!"* We had made it to America. We were all about to understand what that would really mean.

My father had made arrangements for Aunt Anna and Uncle Frank to pick up us from the airport. Uncle Frank was a very conservative gentleman. He was the first in his family to be born in the United States, but he held strictly to the conservative, family-oriented values of Italy. Looking back, I wonder what he thought about having my mother, my father and their four children living under his roof for while.

But, of course, that's what Italian families do. We live for each other, help each other, always ready to give a leg up. That's how we are.

As soon as we could, we bounded off the plane like fireballs. We watched as the adults exchanged their hellos and kisses on the cheek. They spoke in Italian about the flight, the family still living back home and what was going on in America.

As I looked around the baggage claim area, I could see the metal belt sitting still and quiet like silver robotic snake waiting to slither away.

"Look," Sonny said, "that thing is going to start soon. Let's see if we can hitch a ride."

Another Italian family who had been on our flight was already standing by awaiting their luggage. We made our way near to them. They had a couple of kids that were about our size.

"Giulio, I dare you to go over and pull that girl's hair," Sonny pestered as we both eyed her long dark braids.

"Don't be stupid, Sonny. What has she done to deserve that? Let's just wait here. Why would you want to do something like that?" Vin asked.

"Because it would be funny," Sonny said, laughing.

My eyes yo-yoed between the two children. The brother seemed to be eyeing us with a bit of fear. He was outnumbered and he knew it. His sister smiled at the three boys so intently looking at her. Innocent to the thoughts skipping inside our minds, she hugged her rag doll close with one arm and started twirling the end of a braid with the other hand.

Indeed, I agreed with Sonny; it would be kind of funny to see what happened if I pulled her hair. But, I really just wanted to touch it. It was a beautiful. I liked girls. I liked them a lot. Approaching her just to tug on the braid would give me an excuse to get closer to what intrigued me most — girls.

At the same time my thoughts were balanced out by Vin. Flashes of my dad's anger on the plane made me stop and think for a second. "Yeah, what has she done to deserve to be hurt?" More than that, I didn't want my dad to get pissed at me again. Once is enough for one day.

I glanced over my shoulder back at our parents. It seemed that every adult was deeply entrenched in a conversation. This clearly was an opportunity that could not be ignored. Sonny continued to egg me on.

"Come on, just do it. Go over there and give just one little tug. Don't be a chicken."

I looked over to Vin. He had his head down. He looked up at me through his lashes and slightly shook his head back and forth in a silent "No, don't do it."

Sonny wouldn't let it rest. "You can do it!" he whispered. Then louder, "You wanna do it!" *Vai! Vai! Tira! Tira!* "Go! Go! Pull it, pull it!"

The coast was clear and the pressure was building.

"Do it, do it!" Sonny chanted.

My mind raced. My heart pounded. My toes started tapping and before I knew it I was slowly, like a cat on the prowl, approaching the girl. Purposefully I did an eye lock on the girl's left braid. I avoided looking into her face. Closer, closer I drew. I stopped just in front of the two kids. I checked again to guarantee the coast was clear and felt my hand reach out and my gaze slip. I looked into the little girl's eyes and saw horror. I took pity. Without even thinking, I pulled back my elbow and punched her brother in the gut.

A deafening cry sounded an alarm throughout the entire baggage claim area. I prepared myself for some sort of retaliation from the boy, or even his sister. Instead I felt the heavy strength of a man lifting me off the ground by my hair. Back then it was nothing for a parent to backhand their kids in public. Now, they'd be afraid that they'd get arrested for child abuse, but that was a different time.

The man who had taken hold of me was my father. He shook me, spanked my butt and scolded me as I dangled in his grasp. With an edge of pain my bottom was firmly planted on a marble staircase near where the relatives and family friends, now staring at us, were gathered. The adults were looking at my dad with approval, understanding it had to be done that way. It was how Italians handled things.

"What were you doing?" My father half-yelled and half-threatened me as his eyes bulged like a frog. Being looked at like that made me feel like he'd hit me. He was making that distinctive Italian gesture again that told me I was gonna get it.

I looked up at him with a blank stare. I didn't dare answer. The more you answered the more you got.

Uncle Frank had made his way over to us. I thought he might take a swing as well. He was *Itolamericano*. Even though he was born in America, he had retained many of the traditional Italian values and customs. Good for me he'd been Americanized enough to lay off a bit.

"What happened?" My uncle asked my father.

My father held tight — extra tight — to my shoulder. His strong, sharp fingertips bit mercilessly into the tender spot just above my collarbone. The intense pressure was invisible to everyone but me. My father was intentionally slow to describe the event to Uncle Frank, all the while increasing his vice-like grip. He was skilled at making the blood rise behind my ears until they began to ring.

"Vin was right," I thought. "I should have listened. I should NOT have done that. Next time I'm going to take Vin's advice."

And thinking back on that moment, I was sure I would make a better choice next time. Or would I?

As we left the airport in the back of my uncle's car, I thought about what had happened. I was kind of mad at Sonny for egging me on like that. On the other hand, even at the tender age of 5, I also knew that I could have listened to Vin instead of Sonny. Or I could have just done my own thing. I didn't know why I cared about what those two thought of me.

What I did know was I was going to have enough things to deal with in the days ahead. I didn't need advice that was going to get me in trouble. But even as I had the thought, I knew that this was far from the last time.

What I didn't anticipate was how hard the next days were going to be for me: trying to start school in a foreign land, with people I knew nothing about, in a language I didn't understand. How on earth was I going to manage all of this?

3.
No Speak English

My first day of school in America was quite memorable. *Ma non parlo Inglese* was my mantra. My kindergarten teacher, Mrs. Harlow, was nice enough but challenged by me. Vin and Sonny were lucky. They were able to fake it until they made it. Not me. Language, especially the writing and reading, was near to impossible to fake because I just didn't get it.

"Gwell-yoh, uh, Gooellio. Hoolio? Mmmm…Gooolow. AH! How DO you say your name?" The teacher was almost as exasperated as I was. I had no idea what she was saying.

"I think she wants to know how to say your name," Vin explained.

I looked up at her. "Giulio," I mumbled.

"Jew-lee-oh," she replied. It was the last time she was even close. The rest of the school year, I was called everything from Mario to Julio, to her unique Gwell-yoh, to whatever else someone came up with.

So imagine your first day of school: you are all excited and goose-bumpy to be with the other kids and start something new, but you have a dark, pointed, gigantic olive pit poking you in your tummy.

It whispers up from your gut saying, "see? You aren't like the other kids. You are LESS THAN they are." This voice made me feel dumb. I couldn't communicate. I couldn't express myself with words.

I was supposed to bring a blanket to kindergarten for nap time. No matter how I tried to explain this to my mother, no matter how many notes were pinned to my shirt to help me explain it, she didn't understand.

Eventually, to avoid the embarrassment of not having a nap time blanket, I simply skipped that part of kindergarten. Instead of going in after recess for naps, I stayed outside. When the autumn leaves began to turn, I was out there. When the snow began to fall, I was out there. When the snow piled up to snow banks, I was out there sitting on one, waiting out the rest of the day.

I was a tough little tyke. Come on, how many 5-year-olds suffer through the torture of an upstate New York winter afternoon to avoid being embarrassed? I was also not as inventive then as I am now. Perhaps this is one of the compelling factors that helped me become resourceful and find alternative routes through life. The godsend in all of this was that kindergarten was only a half-day.

My teacher and I struggled to communicate. I couldn't seem to pronounce anything right, say anything right or do anything right. Every day brought a new set of frustrations.

One sunny winter afternoon, I had to go to the restroom. Bad. I had held it as long as I could, hoping that the teacher would notice my squirming and the anguished look on my face. Finally, I mustered the courage to go up to her desk.

"Devo andare al bagno."

"Speak English," she said sharply, not even looking up.

"Devo andare al bagno."

I didn't know what she was saying, but I knew what I was saying. Why didn't she understand me?

"I won't be answering you until you say it in English, whatever you're saying."

"Devo andare al bagno!" "Devo andare al bagno!" I was dancing now.

I was holding my pene so hard, I thought I was going to pinch it right off. If she didn't let me go to the bathroom soon, I was going to pee my pants. Right here in front of everybody. I was starting to panic, which didn't help the whole situation.

"Devo andare al bagno!" The tears began to well up.

I just couldn't hold it any longer. Standing at the teacher's desk, trying to communicate my need to go to the bathroom, I did. I peed in my pants.

Just then, the bell rang. I ran out of the room, leaving a trail of wet behind me. Down the empty hallway, past the front office, out the door and all the way home, bawling the whole way.

By the time I got home, I was depleted. I was wet. I was humiliated. I was angry. I was ashamed. I was sad. I was frustrated. I had run the gamut of these negative emotions all the way home. How on earth was I going to make it here? Nobody understood me. I understood nobody. I wanted to go back to Italy.

"Giulio, just listen to what everyone else says and copy them," Vin suggested.

"School is stupid," Sonny chimed in, and I noticed that he stuck with his opinion.

Somehow, I muddled through kindergarten and into first grade. I really thought I was getting the hang of this school thing. I knew my father's charm had rubbed off on me a bit and I smugly thought to myself that I had this knocked out. No problem.

First grade was great. Okay, so I didn't speak much English yet. And I didn't understand very much. But I was picking up some things. At least the teacher didn't seem as frustrated with me as my kindergarten teacher had been. By the end of first grade I'd learned some of the right words — "bathroom," "please" and "paper."

I could tell that my teacher knew I was trying hard, and I was. The first day back at school after summer break, I dress especially nice. I was wearing a red sweater, a white shirt and a bow tie. I remember thinking that I looked nice and I smiled the whole way to school. I took my seat with the confidence that things were going my way. How wrong I turned out to be.

As was the tradition, we returned to our previous year's classroom, for a short program where the teacher highlighted some of the things we had learned that year, and some of the outstanding students that had done so well. It hadn't dawned on me that almost every student had been singled out for some achievement except for me. I hadn't even noticed. As the class rose to be graduated from first grade and moved on into second grade, I was told to sit down.

"What?" I wasn't sure I had heard her right.

The whole class was standing except for me. As my classmates moved toward the door to join their new second grade teacher, I still wasn't quite clear what was going on.

Then the first kid in the line of the new class coming in, Steve DeCarlo, started pointing at me, yelling: "You flunked! You flunked!"

I didn't know what he was saying, but I knew something was wrong. I mean, the whole class I had spent the last year with was leaving and I was staying behind.

Until that moment, when the entire classroom turned around to stare at me, I'd had no clue that I was doing so badly. And I felt powerless and ashamed and stupid. I folded my arms on my desk and I buried my head in them. Maybe if I just pushed really hard, my head would just be swallowed into my desk and I'd never have to look at any of them again. I felt very, very small.

I wanted to hate Steve DeCarlo, but I was too ashamed to hate anybody. Besides, he didn't mean anything by it. It was just so unusual, it kind of shocked everybody. Ironically, Steve became one of my closest friends and stayed my friend throughout my school days and even after.

I never really learned how to read or write properly. In fact, I don't remember writing much at all. I had charm and I was cute, so I think that's how I won my teachers over throughout my school years. They admired the fact that I refused to give up. I had learned the finer points of charisma from my dad, but the other things were secrets from Sonny. Vin was more about helping me and trying to tutor me. He had picked up English very quickly and tried to teach me.

I sure felt like I was thick-headed. I remember feeling confused all the time — there was no clarity for me. Some days it felt like I was swimming through mud.

They sent me to "special ed" classes and an "English as a second language" program. The teachers always talked about how cute I was, and we spent the class time with them asking me how to say words in Italian.

I'd obligingly say "libro" as one of them would hold up a book, and they would collapse into a fit of giggles and "ooohs" and "Oh! He is SO CUTE!" It's no surprise that I didn't learn much English there.

Still, I understood that it was imperative that I finish school. So I cheated. I mimicked. I copied and stole answers. I turned on the charm and the humor whenever it was necessary, and sometimes when it wasn't probably necessary. But when it's the only weapon in the arsenal, that's the one you choose.

It still hurts today, sometimes, as I think about those first school years. The words I most vividly remember are "stupid," "idiot" and "dumb." At the time, I didn't know how to translate the words into Italian but the tone of the teacher's voice told me that I was worthless.

I really did try so hard, and I felt that while other kids had rough starts, too, at least they spoke the language. My self-esteem slowly diminished and my confidence shrank with my inability to complete each written assignment. I was feeling very insignificant, like I hardly made a difference to anyone.

Free yourself from the expectations of others by being true to yourself.

4.

Take It Like A Man

I knew I mattered to my family, but even in the family atmosphere, I felt inferior and belittled. I grew up on American soil but belonged to an Italian family. It was Old World tradition flowing through our veins: our recipes, our conversations, and as you have seen, our methods of parental discipline. My father, just as he was raised, firmly believed that pain deters. I think his exact formula would have been: pain + pain = reformed behavior.

It usually started with spankings and worked its way up to *the belt*. One was expected to stand at attention while being slapped or hit with this leather strap. These were the expectations. And, before you pick up a phone to call family services, get a reality check from any Italian baby boomer you know. This is how it was. Was it an import from Europe? Or just the way of the parent for our generation? I'm not sure. It wasn't considered extreme. It was more of a *tradizione*.

My parents would not intentionally hurt anyone in the world. They had big hearts and they loved us in a huge way. They simply knew no other means by which to raise a family or a boy like myself. Honestly, I preferred the quick painful way rather than being punished by being grounded in my room for days. I took my punishment swift and hard. In fact, I took it so well it was scary. Somehow I found a way to separate from it and go somewhere else in my head to avoid taking the punishment straight on.

Maybe what drove me here was my father's expectation to hear no rebuttal, no whimper, no reaction to what he dealt out. I stood like a man. I took it silently and moved on because in my world the day was mine. I was way more interested in being active and moving on with things. This pattern replayed itself often and resulted in me seeking out the "quick fix" or the "shortcut" to any of my ends.

I was usually in some sort of trouble. Now I know that part of my problem was ADHD. It was rarely talked about when I was a kid yet that's all you hear now. Sometimes I just did things without thinking. And, sometimes I couldn't stop once I started.

For example, I'd come to the dinner table and take my place next to my father. Pretty soon my right foot was tapping, my hands were fidgeting with the flatware and I was whistling. Dad would pop me on the back of my head. There was no need for words. We communicate with our eyes and hands, us Italians. I'd absorb the pop and nod in agreement to the rule and try to knock it off.

Twenty seconds later nature would set in and again my foot would tap, my fingers drum on the table and unconsciously I'd begin to pucker my lips. The first sound of wind started to form a whisper of a whistle while my mind screamed out, "oh shit, you're dead!" I couldn't stop it.

The sound would release and sure enough there came another almighty high-powered, highly effective slap to the head.

"*A posto!*" I thought, stop it. Only his eyes said, "how many times do I have to tell you not to whistle at the table?" And again I'd settle down.

Thirty seconds would pass and the impulse would kick in. Just as my foot started to tap and my lips began forming into an "o," short-term memory failed me, like it never happened before. This was all in an effort to teach us to be proper. My father wanted us to sit properly and straight at the table, to be ladies and gentlemen, to be socially appropriate. Everything that happened at the table in terms of discipline was for a good reason, even if it resulted in a bruise under the chin.

"I hate that one," Sonny said. He pointed to the dark purple smudge-like bruise on the soft skin under my jaw. "Do you just want to punch him out when he grabs you there?"

A grin spread across my face when I heard Sonny talk like this. "Yeah," I said timidly to start with and then more boldly. "Yeah! You're right I just want to hit him."

"Right, even bust his nose!" Sonny encouraged.

"I hate it, too when he pinches me when we're out. He gets a painful finger full of skin right under my arm or my chin. That kills. Nobody sees the impact of it but it kills me like crazy."

"Our parents know it. They also know nobody is going think much about grabbing us like that."

"Right on," I proclaimed as I started to gain emotional momentum. "Sometimes I feel like whipping my elbow out and landing one in the gut to get him to stop."

"Sometimes I want to go just crazy on him, or I wish he would move away or something. One time, I even wished he would get hit by a car because I was so pissed off at him."

My jaw dropped open. It sounded so bad, but I didn't want to admit I had those same wishes sometimes. I mean, what kid didn't, right? But hearing the words out in the open like that was so in my face!

"Giulio, what's wrong ?" Sonny jeered. "You never think about that stuff? Oh come on, I know you do."

"Maybe," I said.

"Well I have," Sonny emphasized. "Sometimes I get so pissed about how they hit us that I think of ways that a kid can fight back. You know, just get even."

This is how far Sonny would go in his head. Of course we would never do anything drastic, but we couldn't help but talk some smack about our parents. Every kid does, I was sure.

Good thing Vinnie wasn't around that day because he may have flipped out over what and how we were talking. It was good for me, though. It was good to be free to hear Sonny out and to take what he said and run it through my mind.

But in reality, I never allowed those thoughts to stay in my head for long. Our parents are the ones who loved us first, you know? It's that unconditional, nurturing love that has kept me going for as long as it has.

As a kid, I felt like I had become the fall guy for the family. It seemed that whenever one of my siblings caused a problem I was the one who was usually punished. Somehow my parents were convinced that I had something to do with most of the mischief in the house.

I was an easy target, a magnet for the blame, because of my natural energy and because I leaned toward Sonny's temperament. I had decided in my own mind, separate from conversations with Vin and Sonny, that I had been hit so much that I was numb. I had found a way to dissociate from the pain and the shame of it all. I was determined to absorb it seemingly unflinchingly. I was prepared to take it. To take it like a man.

Even though this would later become a dangerous game played out on my own self-esteem and confidence, it worked at the time. Even though we look up to our heroes, there's a time in each kid's life that we don't understand them. It changes as we get older, I've found. The things that bewildered me the most when I was growing up, like discipline, are the things that I truly understand the most now. But then, it just made me feel rotten.

Do you know the thoughts that go through a youngster's mind? The places a kid goes to mentally when a parent, sibling, or bully continually inflicts pain? It doesn't matter what type of pain it is — verbal or physical. The fragile child inside me screamed out in pain and in fear. I yelled and rebelled but all in the silence of my mind. Fear crept in because in my small thought patterns I could not know, could not process all the reasons that pain is okay to deal out to your children.

Your hide burns as if touched by a hot iron and you begin to believe that you deserve it. Some kids are disciplined because they lost a football, a skateboard, a bike, their ipod or phone. I didn't have any of these material things to lose. What I lost was the only thing I owned - my sense of self-worth. I came to believe that I must be somewhat flawed or I wouldn't be the scapegoat. I thought something must be a bit defective, or I wouldn't be the object of discipline.

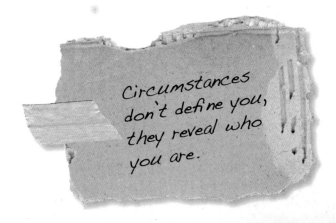

Circumstances don't define you, they reveal who you are.

5.

Fifth Grade Punching Bag

Somewhere along the way I became a target for bullying. I think it's somewhat normal for a kid who believes he's defective in some way. It began October 4th to be specific, which happens to be my birthday. Out of the blue a miserable little kid named Bernie ran at me from behind and knocked me down by tripping my feet out from under me. Then he body-slammed me. Once I was sprawled on the ground trying to gain some idea of what had just happened, he took to punching me in the face several times.

Being much larger than Bernie, I easily pushed him off. I got up, blinked the sun out of my eyes and looked at him in curious wonder. "What the hell was that about?"

It only took a second for Bernie to realize that I wasn't rolling around dumbstruck on the ground. And when he did, he got angry. Angry enough to make a fist and come after me again. Still waiting for him to answer me, I wasn't sure he'd really hit me. This time I took the shot to my face and it drove me to my knees. A dozen kids moved in and circled me.

"Shit," I yelled. I rolled over to notice all the shoes attached to people who wanted to see the fight. However, being encircled like this made me feel trapped. Like dead meat in the middle of a hungry pack, with each waiting to take their turn at the food.

My thoughts were quickly interrupted, however, when Sonny jumped in and fell to the ground next to me.

On his hands and knees he yelled with ear-shattering volume and spit, "Rip his head off Giulio! Take this sucker down! Smash his brains out!"

I looked up again, seeking out Bernie. My search stopped on Vin. There he stood just inside the circle. His arms folded and a firm look that said, "Don't do it Giulio." He even spoke, "This punk isn't worth you getting in trouble."

At that very moment with each voice playing in a separate ear, the shadow of my teacher darkened the sun from my vision.

"Get up Giulo," Mr. LaClair said. All the chatter quieted and a hush fell over the circle of kids. I could hear Bernie's sniffling off to the side like a child who had been caught with his hand in the cookie jar.

I brushed myself off as I stood up. Mr. LaClair put his hands, one on each of our shoulders, directing us toward the school.

"Come on guys," he said. "You are going to have to explain this to the principal."

The way Mr. LaClair looked down at me when he spoke seemed to be asking me, "Why didn't you fight back? Bernie is a scrawny brat who probably deserved it." His eyes looked almost like my father's eyes when they asked questions. And in the stupor of the moment I realized that I didn't have a good answer to this question.

Bernie was actually a bit of a squirt. He had a squirrel-like quality about him with big teeth and uneven hair. He was always mad, always trying to pick a fight with anyone. Looking back, I think he was miserable. At the time I was bewildered by the idea that someone would just want to hurt me for no good reason, especially on my birthday.

I wasn't cool with the idea of hurting someone. Even though parents hit kids, I knew it wasn't right to hurt someone. So I didn't. And now, because of Bernie other smaller kids saw how I resisted. They began taking pot shots at me hopeful that I'd treat them like I had Bernie. I'd absorb the pokes and blows like I did with my father. Every bump, nick and ding hurt no matter how small. This definitely didn't do anything to help my self-esteem.

At lunch, three or four kids would tell me they were gonna kick my ass after school, just to get me to cry. Not that I was scared; I was just so tired of the pain that I knew awaited me. Again.

Sure I hated that I absorbed pain at home and at school, whether it was from my dad or the bullies. There was a difference, though. I knew my dad loved me. I knew he was trying to teach me. However, I couldn't come up with a good reason for the other verbal and physical beatings. Day after day this built up.

Today kids begin to mimic the experience by burning themselves with cigarettes, or they start cutting themselves or they try something else. I really have to admit that even then, even at such a young age, I loved life. I liked being me. I didn't ever want to hurt myself or anyone else. I withstood a lot because of my belief in life itself. I wanted to cry and whimper in a corner, but I didn't want to add to the harm and hurt of the world.

Sonny made it hard to keep my cool, to feel okay about

my decision to not fight. "Coward, you are a sissy," he would chide. "Are you afraid of jail? Are you? Are you afraid to go crazy on someone?"

I know he was teasing, but it stung and this only added to my lack of having a good sense of self.

I often thought about how my father would react in these types of situations — not that he had the same problems I did. He'd found a good job in America. He worked at General Electric. I wasn't sure what he did there but I think it was something with turbines. He always stuck out in the crowd of blue-collar workers with his jacket, tie, and the fedora pulled low over his eye like always. His self-confidence was always in plain view.

The other guys would give him a hard time, and he just seemed to ignore it. "Hey Veglio, you Mafia or what?" The whole group of them would collapse in fits of laughter. He walked with pride and looked classy. He ignored what they had to say.

Sometimes I wondered what violent acts my dad was truly capable of performing. This was a man who had put some very high-powered individuals in jail for tax evasion and fraud in Italy. He never (that I knew of) lowered himself to show them. He was a man of few words. He never had to brag but he never had to worry, either. He had a quiet confidence which I didn't appreciate until I was much older.

Today, I'm grateful that he led by example. I only hope I can pass on that quiet confidence to my kids.

Without self confidence, it is impossible to achieve great results.

Part Two
Growing Up

6.

All The World's A Stage

The confidence I picked up from my dad helped me pave my own way to success. I have more street smarts than most. They were fine-tuned because of my learning disabilities.

Since my reading and writing abilities suffered, I grew up knowing how to position myself in any situation by being able to talk, think creatively and work hard. My achievements have more to do with guts and vision than formal book learning.

And by junior high, I found out quite clearly that I could sing!

Hundreds of hours were spent sitting by the stereo. I'd rig up a homemade microphone and hang it from the chandelier. Down by the railroad tracks, we'd pick up random parts and junk to pretend we had all the expensive equipment we needed. We acquired a cheap semi-working guitar and a completely non-working amp, so in my imagination our living room was a recording studio. Not all of my efforts here were fantasy-based. My singing ability was part of my DNA.

My father had been an incredible singer in Italy. He competed and won many music awards. When he came to the States he was lined up to audition for *The Ed Sullivan Show*. He was that good. In Italy my grandfather insisted that my dad go to college instead of into music. He thought singing was silly.

In America, my father had to choose between taking care of his family and being on television. While family was always first for him, I would have been more selfish!

There are deep pockets of musical talent in our family. I wish I could have been more like my father when playing the accordion, guitar and piano. He could play by ear and hear all the nuances of the music. It was his passion. With his charisma and soul, he could have been a mega-star!

In my idolization of my father, I pretended to be a mega-star myself. If I was messing around mimicking Elvis on the radio, my father would know instantly if I was off key.

"Ascoltare la musica," he would say. "Listen to the music."

If he didn't say anything I knew my pitch was good. If Elvis was jiving to *Blue Suede Shoes* my voice transformed to his. I could mimic any male singer on the radio. Hand me a guitar or any other instrument and I was lost. Allow me to use my voice and I was transformed.

To my good fortune, my sister was dating a young man who was in the Navy. Before he was deployed, he came over and allowed us to borrow his record albums. (I may have accidentally "borrowed" some without actually asking. Sorry!)

Today you'd call them "vinyl" and they'd be collection pieces. Back then they were my lifeline to music. We couldn't afford record albums on our own. My sister and I would act out musicals like *Grease*. She'd become Olivia Newton-John while I was John Travolta and our living room became our stage.

"Giulio, you guys are great," Vin would praise me after my sis and I would take a bow, walking away from a round of *Summer Lovin'* or *You're The One That I Want*. Everybody thought so, and told us both.

I grinned and said, "It's easy when you have the stereo backing you up."

"No I mean it man! You have talent," Vin would go on.

"Yeah like that's going to make a difference with anything," Sonny added.

I could tell he was sour about Vin's enthusiasm. Lately Sonny had become more pessimistic about everything. "It never got your dad anywhere Giulio. Don't let it go to your head."

I knew I could sing. I knew that I had some talent because music felt so good. My voice was on. Singing came easier to me than any subject at school ever had. Music was my escape; it soothed my soul. Yet Sonny's words tucked themselves in a dark corner of my brain and itched away there insuring that I didn't have full confidence at even this.

I was at lunch one day when I overheard some kids at the next table talking about auditions for *Bye, Bye Birdie*, the next school musical.

Vin leaned over smiling. "Giulio, you should go sign up to try out! You're the best singer I've ever heard," he said enthusiastically.

Sonny, his usual self was quick to shoot holes in the idea. "No way man. He doesn't have the guts for it."

"That's it," I thought to myself. "I'm gonna show him. I'm gonna show everybody." I immediately got up and went outside the cafeteria where the sign up sheets were. I was gonna do it.

I was disappointed to see that the sign up sheets were already full. As I stood there, thinking about how I'd blown another opportunity to build myself up a bit, I must have looked pretty dejected, because one of my teachers came up behind me.

"You thinking about trying out?" He asked. I turned and looked at him with a disappointed response. "I really wanted to sign up and at least try out, but the sheet is already full."

He peered over my shoulder and saw that it was, indeed, full. He said, "So it is, so it is. Well, maybe next time."

In my mind I could hear him saying, "Sure, Giulio can play a little football and maybe his voice is not too bad, but the kid doesn't excel in anything here. How could he pull off a role in our play?"

I went back into the lunchroom and told the guys the auditions were full. I really was disappointed. I knew there were things I couldn't do, but I could pull off singing, that's for sure. Everybody said so. Everybody except of course Sonny.

We all know people like this — people who have talent or special skills who let someone like Sonny hold them back.

Vin always encouraged me. "Yeah, if you don't try you never get anywhere, Giulio. At least you went out there to try. I know you can sing. You don't need permission from your school to be a singer."

About a week passed and while I was tapping my foot and watching the clock in Algebra 1, the music teacher came to the door. The whole class watched the door open. The music teacher popped his head through the doorway, scanned those of us in the room and waved Mr. Waite over. My old knee-jerk reaction triggered and I felt like I was a fifth grader again and about to be hauled into the principal's office. To my surprise, I wasn't going to the office. But the music teacher did want me.

"Giulio, things are not working out so well in our play. I'm wondering if you'd audition for me. We still need more male singers."

Inside, I just wanted to jump up and hug the guy, I was so thrilled. But I had to stay cool, so I casually said, "sure." I had a million thoughts racing through my mind. I wondered what part they needed help with! I wondered what they had been doing that hadn't worked!

I walked into the music room for my spontaneous audition and came face to face with the 52,000 music students from that period. Well, okay, it was really just 52, but it seemed like 52,000!

"Okay Giulio," the teacher directed. "Stand behind the podium and let's see what you can do with *One Last Kiss*."

One Last Kiss? That's the song for the LEAD! I'm trying out for THAT???

"Sure," I said half with disbelief and half cavalier like a charming, self-confident rock star. I hadn't had time to worry or think. I just showed up as I am on the inside. I took my place at the podium and that's when my knees began to tremble. "Oh man," I thought. "What if I botch this? What if I'm off key?"

As thoughts of my dad's high standards and Sonny's criticism were floating through me, I anchored into how I felt singing at home with my sis. It felt good. I remembered Vin's encouragement and took a deep breath, ignored my shaky legs and started right on cue.

"*Oh, one last kiss,*" my head was clearing. "*Give me one last kiss,*" my voice was strong. "*Give me one last kiss.*" I was Conrad and the room disappeared.

"*It never felt like this, No, never felt like this. You know I need your love. Oh! Oh! Oh!...*" My knees were moving behind the podium but now they were doing that Elvis thing I did so well at home. My eyes were closed, my face pointed to an imaginary rigged up microphone hanging from the chandelier.

"*Ba-a-a-a-a-a-a-aby-y-y, give me one last kiss!*" I opened my eyes and saw a room full of dropped jaws, broad smiles and popping eyeballs. The class liked it! They liked it!

I went back to belting out, "*Oh, give me one last kiss! One last kiss, one last kiss, Oh, give me on last kiss!*" And the music stopped. Girls squealed, guys high-fived, I blinked and looked at the music teacher.

"Giulio, you'll be Conrad Birdie in our play. Rehearsal starts right after school today. Don't be late."

The rest of the day pretty much seemed like a dream. The 52 students in the music room were blown away. I was blown away. The news of how I pulled it off traveled as fast as light speed on speed. All I remember were the voices and the slaps on the back. All the faces were blurred.

"You were amazing!"

"Where did you learn to sing like that?"

"Hey man, that was cool! You sound better than Elvis."

I went to rehearsal that night in a daze, and that's why I may have over-promised what I could deliver. When I went home I not only had the lead role, I also had volunteered my mom to make my costume.

Good thing my dad worked for a top clothing designer as his second job that he did in the mornings before his shift at GE and was allowed, from time to time, to bring home patterns. My sisters had homemade jeans that ran side by side with the hottest label in town — Jordache. Good thing I was Italian. When I asked for my family to help on a worthy cause, nothing would have stopped them. In fact, my mother, her friends and my sisters all pitched in.

Not even a week passed and I had the perfect costume. You can imagine it right now. It was a silver jumpsuit with a zipper that went all the way down to there, silver sparkly trim and full-on silver belt with a dazzling buckle. The bell-bottoms and the platform boots put the cherry on the top. I looked like a million bucks. I felt even better.

When I was on stage I was a ladies man, I was the cool guy, I was Conrad. I have no idea where Giulio hung out during rehearsals and the actual play. I was who I always wanted to be, and who I saw myself as when I looked at myself with non-judgmental honesty. I was brilliant. All my insecurities were pinned down. My buddies watched from their auditorium seats but I didn't take too much time to check out what they had to say about everything that was going on. I just wanted to bask in my moment of glory, and bask I did.

There were kissing scenes. I could flirt my head off on stage, and I did. Girls from all over the school were swooning over me during lunch and in the hall. When the play opened for its two-week stint, even girls from other schools would say "hi" to me in town or hang out of their cars to wave at me if they saw Vin and Sonny and I outside a pizza joint. There were little girls from grade school, and sometimes even little boys, who wanted me to sign their autograph books.

I didn't invite my parents to watch the play. Dad was busy with work and I was relieved to know he wouldn't be coming. I was more nervous to hear what he might say about my performance than any other living being.

What if he said I was awful? What if something happened and I messed up. I couldn't live with the thought of having my perfect pitch father see me make an error. Not on the stage; not where he was king.

My mom had the home to tend to and children to watch after. She needed to be home to support my father when he came home for dinner, so I faced the pressure of opening night on my own. It was full of pressure, but somehow I got up and transformed into my role even better than I had in my audition. I made it through that night with flying colors, and the next, and the next as well. I was a hit, a rock star for that one moment and I knew in my blood how it felt to be at the top of your game.

Even though this experience sent me right to cloud nine, something — my lack of self-confidence I now believe — stopped me from trying out for another play again. My mind raced every time the topic came up.

Vin would elbow my shoulder and encourage me. "Giulio, you blew us all away. People are still talking about it. Go for it!"

Then Sonny would say, "look Giulio, you know you can do Elvis, you can do Andy Gibb, but at some point your luck is going to run out." I must have listened to Sonny more than Vin because the only other ego boost I got was when I was asked to sing at high school graduation. I picked Andy Gibb's *Shadow Dancing*.

It's funny, though, looking back on that experience, you move close to what you focus on. Focus on what you want, and you will get it. At that moment, when I was on stage, I could be whoever I wanted. I could be, and I WAS, great. It was interesting, though, because even though I was great at that play and at that time, Sonny's words of discouragement were so firmly lodged in my brain that I never allowed myself to explore the possibility of doing another play. I figured it was best to quit while I was ahead.

I just couldn't get past the lack of confidence in order to make my life. But the risk I had taken by being the lead in *Bye, Bye Birdie* had really been great! Why couldn't I allow myself those feelings again? What stopped me? Why wouldn't I push myself just a little bit harder?

Ultimately, my fear of failure won over my potential for future acting and singing success. It's too bad, because I'd done a really good job on that play. Still, it did have its benefits. I became "somebody" if only for a moment, especially with the girls.

Never let fear of failure stop you.

7.

Treat The Girls With Style

Success with the girls, however, was a different story. I did have a fear of failure with girls, of course. What teenager doesn't? But in my mind, I was larger than life. I was a romantic at heart, and girls said I had a way with the ladies.

Apparently, like my father was in his day, I was "hot" in the minds of many, many girls. Somehow I missed this fact in high school. What I can tell you is that I was painfully aware of and on constant vigilance against the possibility of looking foolish. I was horrified at looking stupid. When you're on constant guard your real self gets locked out. That was me in high school — only half alive.

Vin didn't care what anyone thought of him, including the girls. He was the freest of us all. Sonny was kind of a pig - the guy who couldn't get enough. He was the raunchy comedian, the Andrew Dice Clay of the group — no couth, too forward, always embarrassing.

I was more "normal" in the sense that I didn't want to look weak or come across poorly in front of girls. I played it cool. You know the gig — you are aloof to be guarded. You are reserved and semi-approachable because you're scared shitless that you watch everything that moves in case it is a threat to your ego. What kept me from fully enjoying my "hot" status was my desire to be a gentleman.

I learned from the contemporary romantics how to be a gentleman. Stars like Clark Gable and Frank Sinatra showed me how to treat the girls. Dean Martin would sing to the girls from the balcony, like my dad would do. Imagine singing on someone's balcony today — you'd get arrested for disturbing the peace! Especially with today's music! Rap songs by artists named things like Sir-Mix-A-Lot and songs that talk about booties *(I like big butts and I cannot lie!)* just can't compete with the old goodies.

Old classic movies like *Singin' in the Rain* and *An American in Paris* were my training videos. Trust me. Watch old Rock Hudson and Gene Kelly classics and you'll know what I mean.

I also learned the art of being a gentleman from watching my dad respect my mom. He treated her like a lady and I understood that that's how to be. And, I had sisters who taught me how to appeal to women.

"Don't say that, Giulio, it will turn her off," they always admonished.

And I listened.

Yet with my ego in the basement, I got caught up short (and I don't mean sexually). That part can come easy to most guys. What I mean is that I didn't learn how to make a pure connection with another person. Even more harmful was the fact that I didn't learn to connect to myself first, therefore I was clueless to my own value.

Here's how it played out: instead of talking honestly and openly with girls, Sonny and I snagged each other into teenage games. "Sonny," I'd direct: "Go find out, if you can, what 'so and so' says about me."

Or he'd say, "Giulio, check it out. See if 'such and such' would go out with me." Duh! We were so insecure and Vin never seemed like that.

"Get over it," he'd say. "Just be yourself. Girls are people just like you. Talk to them. You'll know if someone likes you. And who cares if they don't? There are plenty of girls out there, so why waste time with the girls who can't see how cool you are?"

I wish, oh how I wish I could have been more like Vin. I wasted so much time groveling in my own black hole where I believed that something was fundamentally wrong with me.

Some of the things that kept my insecurity running wild were the stories I'd weave inside my head. I remember a number of times when I walked past a circle of girls in the halls and noticed how they would stop talking. They'd turn and look at me and start to giggle.

I interpreted this to mean they were laughing at me. Is it my shirt? Are my pants okay? Maybe my hair looks funny?

Of course I thought it was something wrong with me. But if you take time to study the female, particularly those in high school, you would know that this is what girls do when they are nervous - they giggle. Had I been aware I would also have noticed that I made them nervous enough to giggle. If I only knew then what I know now...wow!

Looking back at my high school pictures, I wish I could have stopped my inner critic from taking the wind out of my sails. I actually had a decent track record. I was asked by the most popular girls to junior and senior proms all during 10th, 11th, and 12th grade. Thanks to my paper route, I could afford a tux even in 10th grade. I outclassed most of the other guys in financial matters every time.

There is something I must make clear: there was passion and a high-powered Italian libido attached to my personality. Despite my low self-confidence, don't think that I was abnormally humble and under-experienced sexually. Once I got the green light to move in, I did with bravado. I was a true romantic. The wining and dining, the singing, the flowers — I sure knew how to pour it on.

And this is my point: like so many others who can be good at the "romance" stage of dating, we are not necessarily good at actual relationships. We get stuck in that red alert stage that movies and songs are written to describe — the heart pumping, endorphin-charged passionate attractions! You're high. You are exalted in a state of bliss for anything from six minutes to six months. Then you better have more to your repertoire or you're finished. Well, I was finished.

I didn't know how to get close to another person beyond that point where your self-esteem issues, trust issues, body-image issues overcome the dreamlike state of the beginning.

I would be out with my girlfriend and things were going fine, and my fear would shift into gear. My mouth would open up and I'd say,

"Sure you like me now but pretty soon you're going to see that I'm fat."

"Oh, Giulio, you're not fat. Get over it. You're strong and sturdy. I like how you're built. You're cute, Giulio."

And then I'd go leading with my worst nightmares and say something equally destructive, such as, "you think I'm cute now, but you'll start to notice that my nose is too big and then…."

47

She'd laugh, look at me even closer to see if I was telling the truth about my nose, and then the seeds were planted. Off her pretty little brain would go, watching for more and more evidence that what I was telling her about my ugly duckling factor was true. Pretty soon she started to believe all the stuff I was feeding her and off she'd go to find someone better. I even had one girl simply break up with me because she was tired of me putting myself down. I don't blame her. I could plant abandonment and sabotage seeds so well that they'd sprout in record time.

But I was a master at fishing for compliments like that. We do this subconsciously to get a compliment. Then, when they do compliment us, we question their sincerity! Why do we do this? Today, I've learned to just say "thank you" and enjoy it. I no longer question the motives or doubt the sincerity. But that skill wasn't learned overnight. It started with my "mystery girl."

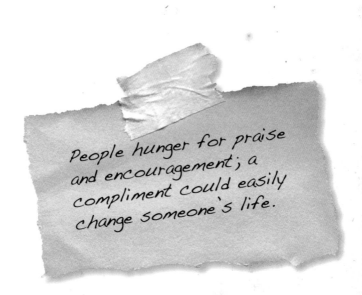

People hunger for praise and encouragement; a compliment could easily change someone's life.

8.

Backstage Rendezvous

The first one to open my heart and let me see my own personal power reflected in her actions toward me was a young woman I call my "mystery girl." She drew me in, touched me deeply, then disappeared. But her mark never did.

Her influence on me started one afternoon after school. She and I just hung out by our lockers until the conversation turned to the school play that interested us both.

"Have you seen the new props for the play?" She asked, flashing her captivating blue eyes at me and shaking her hair over her shoulder as she put her books into her locker.

Dazzled by this quick motion I almost forgot to respond. "Ah, no. Have they started building the set?"

She smiled at my question and melted me. Closing her locker she faced me and said, "let's go look."

She reached down and firmly took my right hand. That touch, that firm and direct contact with her skin sent a sexual charge from my head to my weakened knees. And with that energy beginning to pulse between us, she pulled me with her toward the auditorium.

Everything was dark except for the red glowing *EXIT* letters above a variety of doors. My eyes couldn't see but my memory knew the auditorium well. I pictured the rows of seats on each side and the carpet under my feet as my partner led me to the risers that led up to the main stage. My eyes were just now starting to adjust enough so that I could see her form in front of me, and when we reached the top of the stage she stopped. She turned to face me and her eyes picked up the slightest glow from the exit signs.

She sent chills down my spine when she placed her fingers gently on the back of neck. Oh my God, my heart began to race.

She reached for my hand and delicately pulled me up to the stage curtain until I was lost in the heavy velvet. "Count to three and then come to me," she leaned near my ear and whispered.

I turned my head and asked, "what?" But she was gone.

I didn't wait to count to three. I started grappling with the heavy folds of the curtain with no luck. I finally reached down by my feet, pulled myself an entrance and went under the barrier.

"Where is she?"

There was an ego to protect here and since I was allowing her to make all the rules I remained silent until I tripped over a wooden crate and knocked into a ladder. Lucky for me I was quick and athletic enough to right the ladder before it tumbled.

I knew she was watching all of this because her giggle revealed her position. I immediately turned back toward the front of the stage.

I thought, "she has been right behind the curtain all along."

The rustle of her moving clothing told me she was gone before I got there. I heard her feet running up the aisle on the far side of the auditorium, and I headed in that direction as fast as I could.

The same carpet that led me to the stage was now leading me on a return trip to the audience entrances that led to the school halls.

I was halfway up the auditorium when her angelic voice called my name, "Giulio."

My feet stopped so quickly that I almost tripped myself. I stood still, hoping she would call to me again. She did.

I turned to my left and reached out to steady myself between two rows of chairs. I was getting a little weak in the knees, if you know what I mean. If I broke the silence with words, I believed that the spell would be broken and what was turning out to be a dream come true would actually become more of a dream.

"Giulio," she said again with that sexy voice.

I knew I was close. I moved down the row of chairs on my right very slowly. Halfway in, my knee brushed her leg and she said, "well hello."

I was a flustered mass of hormonal energy and I reached down and touched her legs holding her gently in her seat until I had fully arrived in the seat next to hers.

She placed her hands on my shoulders, ran her hands down my arms and whispered, "you are perfect. I love your strength."

I wasn't quite sure what I had heard, but I knew that I believed every bit of it. For the first time,

I really felt that a girl admired something in me.

She pulled me to her while I put my arms around her shoulders. She looked at me intently and said, "you are powerful. I like that about you. You're very gentle but tough in such a manly way."

In the dark, with nothing more than her words and touch, I was able for the first time to internalize what she was saying. I began feeling myself believe in my own power. Of course she was stroking my ego and in a way that was the perfect language for soul. What more could I have asked for?

She let me hold her for another moment and I finally released her, knowing intuitively she had more in store for me and didn't want things to culminate here. She stood and made her way to the far end of the row. I quickly darted down the row toward the tunnel that led to the green room. I sprinted in that direction, covering several yards in seconds, and slowed down to work my way down a flight of precarious stairs.

At the bottom I had to stop to catch my breath before entering the green room under the stage. I could sense her. I could smell her strawberry lip-gloss. It was if she was floating in the air.

Right when I took a step toward the makeup counters lined against the back wall of the room, she grabbed me from behind. I curbed a yelp and resorted to letting out a single, "hey!" Then she was gone again.

I tip-toed to the back of the stage where all the burly, heavy velvet curtains had been pulled, and slowly felt my way toward where I suspected she was hiding. Moments before I touched, she sprang free from the drapery and jumped on me, knocking me to the floor.

We tumbled and rolled gasping for breath and groping here, then there. Her hair was on my face and my chest but somehow she broke free and left me in a heap, sweating with excitement and a passion my young bones had not ever experienced to this point. Then she evaporated again.

The next day, I couldn't wait to get to the lockers where we had met yesterday. My heart sunk a little as I rounded the corner of the lockers and the hall was empty. I had a feeling I'd find her in the auditorium; at least I hoped I would.

The auditorium was dark again, and it didn't look or sound like there was anyone in there. I walked slowly down the first aisle, by the dim light of that red glowing exit sign, hoping she was there somewhere.

I got nearly to the first row of seats and I was about to turn when I heard that giggle again. I ran for the stage where the curtains were rustling, then up the stairs. The game began again, and ended much the same way as it had the day before, leaving us both breathless and giddy.

This went on for days, until one day, one of us didn't show up. I don't remember now if it was her or it was me, if there was a reason, or there wasn't. But I do remember the impact she had on me — the lasting effect of someone appreciating me for who I am. She didn't see my flaws, my imperfections. She just saw me, a strong, beautiful man.

For years I have looked for her hair, her laugh, her look in the light of day. I have scanned city streets, walkways and crowded halls. Vin and Sonny didn't treasure the opposite sex like I did. Neither of them had a mystery girl, but thank God I did.

I'll never forget the smell of her strawberry lip gloss, or the taste of it on her full, tender lips. She didn't see fat or noses. Whatever she saw I'll never know for sure but that experience helped me to believe that I was wanted.

So whenever I needed to access a voice that would inspire me, it would be hers.

In my imagination she would say, "Giulio, you are incredible! You are special. You are an adorable man!"

And I would soak her words up like toast in soup

until I was soggy and saturated with a warm feeling of being enough. In my dreams I would hold her and kiss her and thank her from the bottom of my heart because for the first time in my life I knew the touch of a first love and it strengthened me. At least, it was a start toward strengthening me.

Ciao, ciao, Bambina. I will never forget.

9.
Most Likely To Charm

Although my struggles with self-confidence still plagued me, I was buoyed by the thought that someone out there thought more of me than I thought of myself.

And, even with those struggles, I did have the right personality, which served me well in my quest to get through school.

One of the miracles of my life was graduating from high school. As I mentioned earlier, getting decent grades and making it academically was impossible for me. I failed or nearly failed on a weekly basis. There are several aspects of the miracle of making it through public education that I have to acknowledge.

Most important, I was very good at telling my

teachers the truth. Teachers like it when you are honest with them. When your back is against the wall and you have no escape, truth and humility are your friends. As a kid with a learning disability, I had to face this early on.

And when I was beat, I had to admit it by stating something like this: "Look, I can't understand this formula but if you'll give me 50 other problems to solve, I'll do that."

Persistence was key. How could a teacher fail a kid who was willing to stay after class, tell the truth about his shortcomings and never give up trying? I put forth every effort I could make, even if it wasn't exactly what my teachers wanted me to do.

In addition to those qualities, charm was at the core of my delivery. It was my ticket. I never resorted to insolence or disrespect.

One night I stayed in my seat in the second row of my math class after all the other kids were gone and all the other teachers were on their way home. Sometimes I was held in situations like this and sometimes I kept myself.

On this night I just looked at my teacher, with anger boiling under my skin and charm oozing out of the pores, and stated my case. "I need you to curve me up to a D so I'm willing to stay here and do extra problems that you know will challenge me, but that I can do. Can we do that? Please?"

Vin would cheer me on when I stayed after. When he could, he would help me by tutoring me. "You can do this, Giulio. You are smart, just not how teachers need you to be when we are in school. But you are smart. Let's get this work done so we can go have some fun."

Sitting by my side to help pass my tests wasn't practical, nor would Vin ever do anything unethical, so I failed at tests on a regular basis.

Sonny was sour about my situation. Hell, he was

sour about everything at this point. He wanted me to manipulate the situation.

"Just do what I do Giulio, buy test answers," Sonny instructed. "It is easy. You don't need to mess around playing games, just cheat your way through. Teachers are suckers. They don't need to know what you know, they just want to grade a handful of papers and pass out judgments with a BIG RED F for failure."

It would have been easy, but it wasn't right. I had a strong belief against cheating, stealing or lying. It's how I was raised. And the thing about lying, cheating and stealing is that they always catch up to you. Trust me when I say this. I have seen so many people lose everything due to their dishonesty. The teachers knew what I was capable of and cheating on tests would have made them suspicious. Besides, I wasn't sure enough about myself to do anything but listen to Vin, my own good conscience.

As mentioned above, I was full of anger and charm. My anger came from feeling trapped inside an IQ that didn't fit in regular classrooms. It came from years of feeling like I was not good enough. I always felt that I was less than everyone. I was weary, mad and discouraged. Yet at the same time, I had a natural love for people. This gentle nature of my heart wanted to win people over and make peace.

"Please, Mrs. North, I know I failed the essay test. I can stay after school. What do you say? I'm willing to work hard for you." My anger made me push back and fight for those D's that I couldn't earn. My charm, my sincerity, my perseverance were what won their hearts and got me through the hurdles of grades K to 12 (including twice in first grade).

What saddens me the most is that I was never dumb. I was just told I was dumb so often that I really believed it. I could read and write and spell but I just didn't know it yet. If teachers were as good at encouragement as they were at put downs (especially with that big red pen) I, like many others, would have felt like I had a chance.

On the other hand, if I had just chosen not to listen to those negative voices that tore apart my self-confidence regularly as a kid, I might not have had such a steep mountain to climb to achieve what I have.

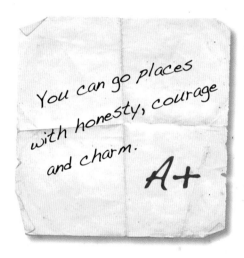

Part Three

Hills & Valleys

10.

Failing My Way To Success

Other voices, both positive and negative, are all around us. Although there was every good reason why I wouldn't be able to finish high school, I did. I just had to make the best of what I had and put it to good use. And to my amazement, I graduated.

I'm fairly addicted to adrenaline and crave it in many forms. How I got talked into going to college though is beyond me. Maybe I listened to Vin more than Sonny for once. Of course the fact that GIRLS, and MORE GIRLS were promised at college was part of the attraction.

Getting in was fairly easy, too. Since I had the car, and I had smart friends who didn't have one, they were willing to help me in exchange for rides. There wasn't mass transit at that time to Schenectady County Community College, in Schenectady, New York. Every morning we'd carpool, park near the student union and head in the direction of our first class. Of course, in Sonny's and my case, eventually we just made a beeline to the game room or student lounge.

But as grade school and high school were challenging, they were nothing compared to college. It was really, really hard, but the girls were hot.

I made a feeble attempt to attend most of my classes at first. Before I knew it I fell so far behind that it seemed to be kind of a futile effort to even continue.

One sunny afternoon, several students were hanging out in the game room. I was stretched out on the couch by the huge windows that overlooked campus, and I was deep in thought.

Vin was actually enjoying college. He had found his niche. He soared in scholastics and was an amazing athlete, too. The things we teased him about when we were younger, like being a "geek" or being a "know it all," were now the things that were making him a success. Sonny and I were finding college life deeply unsatisfying.

"Giulio," Vin semi-whispered, sensing my stare and pulling me out of my daze.

"Yeah?"

"Are you coming to wrestling practice this afternoon?"

"No, I have too much, uh, homework to do, man. How am I going to keep up with school and sports at the same time?"

Sports were the part of college I did enjoy, so it's no surprise that I did much better in that arena than I did in academic pursuits. I did make the wrestling team, and somehow finagled my way into announcing the basketball games. I loved hearing my own voice echo through the gym as I boldly announced a player's name and "two points" as a basket was made. I didn't know much else about basketball, but it didn't seem to matter. My popularity increased with each game and people, especially girls, began to take notice of me.

People (and girls) were noticing that I held my own on the wrestling team, too. It was a good outlet for me, and I liked the matches. I felt powerful as I maneuvered skilled opponents to the mat for the "pin." I wished I could make it through college by participation. I was starting to realize, though, that participation or charm notwithstanding, I was going to have to face reality sooner or later.

I could feel Vin's desire to tutor me and drag me along with him despite the difficulty I was having. I loved him for trying. By now I had learned the hard way that even with Vin's best efforts I might wash out in the end anyway. Vin reassured me with a friendly, agreeing gesture and said nothing more as he returned his attention to his book.

What I was ashamed to tell him is that Sonny and I had already spoken about the possibility of dropping out. We'd agreed that when Vin took off for his study group, Sonny was going to join me in the game room to figure out what we wanted to do. No one knew it, but this had been our "MO" for days.

Sure, we'd meet at the game room. But instead of making plans that afternoon, or any afternoon, about changing direction and doing something constructive, we would hang out with girls watching *General Hospital* in the background. Looking back, I realize that I could tell you more about Luke and Laura's wedding than about anyone or anything else happening on campus.

Sonny and I had already tanked at midterms, since we didn't even go to half of them. I don't know why I continued to try for academic success when I had failed at it my entire life. I really began to question why I had agreed to even try college when I knew it was hopeless. Sure, the girls were great, but I really did not think we were going to be able to make it through.

Since Sonny and I seemed to be avoiding the subject, I decided to take the high road and talk to Vin. I felt that it was only right that I let him know what was going through my mind. I wished things were different. I wished that I was better at reading and writing.

I wished, I wished, I wished, I wished that I didn't have to talk to Vin! He was going to be so disappointed. I could understand that because I was disappointed in myself. But it didn't make sense to continue to beat my head against the wall. I decided that the next chance I had, I would talk things through. But I wasn't looking forward to it.

The wrestling team had an away match. After the match, which we won, Vin and I settled in to our seat near the back of the bus. As the initial jostling and joking subsided, I rehearsed in my mind how I was going to tell him what I was thinking.

Vin broke the silence. "You're awfully quiet."

"Yeah."

"Classes aren't going so well for you, are they?"

"Vin, I don't think I can keep this up. High school was one thing, but this is so much harder. There's no talking my way around things here."

Vin nodded. Though he knew the answer, he had to ask the question. "I thought you wanted to go to college?"

In high school we had plotted and schemed to go to Harvard, but when it came time to make the decision, the money just wasn't there. And, let's be realistic — the chance of me ever getting into any college but a community college with the grades I had just wasn't going to happen. My mom and dad had even dared to hope I'd go to medical school or law school.

And I knew better. "I do, Vin. I did. I just think that some people aren't cut out for college. I can't even make it through the first semester. I don't think seven years of college is going to work out so well."

"So what are you going to do?" Vin's disappointment was evident.

"I don't know, buddy. I don't know."

All the way back to the game room, I asked myself the same question. What I wanted to do was to be an actor or a singer — now that would be cool! But I didn't have any idea how to start that process. Besides, Sonny was always telling me I wasn't any good at that stuff. And there was no WAY my parents would ever go for that.

The next day, Sonny met me in the game room as I pretended not to be interested in *General Hospital*. "Sonny, we've gotta figure out our next step. School isn't working out for us."

"You're right," he said. "I've been thinking about it since we talked about it the other day."

"Got any ideas?" I asked.

"Well," Sonny said slowly. "I was thinking maybe we could join the Army or something."

"Army," I repeated incredulously. "What on earth made you think of that?"

"Hey, it's not such a bad idea," he defended himself. "I thought it would be cool to be MPs and arrest people and stuff! Girls love a guy in uniform. I've heard that a bunch of times!"

Sonny's idea was starting to grow on me as we sat there. I pictured us riding in those jeeps, looking sharp in our MP uniforms. It just might work. I knew that I somehow needed to get myself a trade. Maybe I could be a cop after getting out of the Army.

I decided then and there to check it out at the recruiter's office. I got out the phone book and found the nearest office. I called and asked to speak with a recruiter.

My heart sank as the recruiter told me what was required to enlist — more reading and writing: assessment tests, intelligence tests — just what I wasn't good at — tests. Plus, he said I would be required to bring in all my educational transcripts and grade reports.

"Here we go again," I thought. "I'm not even good enough to get into the Army." I walked out of the game room. I needed some alone time. NOW.

Sonny's bewildered shouts followed me all the way down the hall. "What? What did he say? Where are you going?" I paused before turning the corner. I shouted back, with the exasperation I felt tingeing my voice, "Army's out! What's your next bright idea?"

Vin and Sonny showed up at my table in the cafeteria about an hour later. Sonny said," what do you mean Army's out?"

Vin quizzed, "Army, huh?"

Sonny said, "you know, we were thinking about options and this one came up. If we could train to be cops, like MPs or something, then we'd have a career after."

Vin absorbed what Sonny had said. "You know, this could be pretty good. You know, the military can teach discipline and whip you into shape."

"Yeah, we were really thinking about it," I said sadly. "But I don't think it's gonna work."

"Why not?" Sonny and Vin asked in unison. I was ashamed to even share my doubts with these guys, and they had been through thick and thin with me. It was the same old story. I'd be on a path to somewhere and those doubts and fears rose up in me and overwhelmed me with sadness and shame.

Even my parents didn't believe in me. They never missed an opportunity to tell me about how I should be like my brother. I wished I could be more like Giuseppe. He was a good student and had plans to go to medical school. I wanted their approval so badly.

"It will work, Giulio," Sonny said. "Don't worry about it."

I stood up and threw out that good old Italian gesture angrily. "It WON'T work, Sonny, and the reason is because I am stupid when it comes to reading and writing and they make you take tests and stuff to get in. I won't be able to pass them!" I sank back into my chair, feeling defeated. Again.

Minutes that seemed like hours passed before anyone said anything.

Finally, Vin spoke. "I'll bet you can, Giulio," he said. "Joe Greco just signed up and he said they have tests, but they're all multiple choice and they're easy. You can probably guess your way in."

I still had doubts, of course, but that did make me feel slightly better. Maybe I COULD do it.

"See, Giulio? See? We are gonna look great in those uniforms! Girls won't be able to keep their hands off us! Let's go down there tomorrow."

The next day found Sonny and me skipping classes again and going to the Army recruiter's office. As I walked in the front door, a guy in uniform greeted me. He introduced himself and I remembered he was the man I had spoken with the day before.

I explained that we were interested in what the Army had to offer. I wanted to become "an MP" so I could maybe be a cop after I got out. He assured me that was quite possible, and explained the process to enlist. I made an appointment to come back a few days later to take the tests.

I left that office with a pit in my stomach. I had a strong feeling that those tests were going to trip me up big time. There was no charming my way through this one.

Turns out I was right. Again.

Sonny and I went and took those tests. Of course it was easy for him — he didn't even look at any of the questions, which is why he failed every test! He didn't even try. I was able to pull off the math test all right, but the English and language tests were too hard for me. I just couldn't get through them.

Now what?

After the fiasco at the Army recruiter's office, I knew it was time to make a change. The Army wasn't going to work and neither was college. As much as I wanted to succeed in college, I knew it was time to move on.

As we returned to campus, we decided we'd drop out now since we only had incompletes, not failures. I'd failed at enough already. What I have learned now, though, is that failures are not necessarily bad, they are just learning experiences. You'd think I'd be able to have an honorary college degree, with all those "learning experiences."

There is only one perspective to listen to faithfully — yours!

11.
A Hairstylist?
Are You Serious?

My father looked at me with his disappointed eyes. I'd have preferred a slap on the back of my head than those eyes that he gave me as I told him that college wasn't working out and I'd decided to drop out.

I worked at various places, trying to find my way. As I put on the McDonald's uniform or the construction work boots, I dreamed about the future. I always knew I'd work for myself somehow. I just had to figure out where and how and what.

Before my mother had met my father, she was a hairdresser's apprentice in Italy. She had actually received her diploma as a hairdresser. One day, she casually talked to me about the possibility of me being a hairstylist. She told me that hairstylists can work for themselves and I was pretty creative. I was also really good with people, especially women.

She wanted me to take a tour of the local hairstyling school, but I couldn't picture myself as a hairdresser. I figured my friends would really pick on me.

But, to make mama happy, I agreed to take a tour of the school.

To be honest, I thought cutting hair looked kind of cool. The flair the hairstylists used and the whole "before and after" concept really appealed to me. Besides, mama said that I could get licensed really fast, and fast was my thing.

Sonny freaked when I told him. "No," he yelled. "Everyone will think you're gay!" It was something that bothered me a bit. The few male hairstylists I had met did seem a bit effeminate.

Vin was encouraging. He said that maybe that was exactly what I needed — to work with my hands and learn a trade rather than try so many different ways to get a formal education.

Mama took me to the school for the tour. As we walked through the doors, Sonny changed his tune.

"Holy Moly!" He exclaimed quietly as we walked through the front doors. "I've never seen so many pretty girls in the same room in my whole life!"

An incredibly sexy female voice came from behind us. "Hey, are you coming to school here?"

Without hesitation I answered, "yes, yes we are."

On the way home, we cranked up the radio and sang at the top of our lungs, kissing mama left and right. She thought we were all excited about hair school, but Sonny and I were all excited about GIRLS!

So I started learning about hairstyling. The owners of the school took a liking to me. I guess I charmed them a bit, but it wasn't a manipulative charm. I really liked them, too. Still, it didn't hurt to have them on my side with this whole schooling thing. They found ways to help me pass without so much written work. In return I did things like make their coffee and run errands for them.

The other students were great, too. And pretty. There were some definite benefits to being one of the few males in a school like this! It seemed like I had found a world where I was loved. After feeling so inadequate and worthless for so long, it was refreshing to feel like I had a chance.

I began going out at night and partying way too late with my friends. Many an afternoon found me sleeping under the hair dryer at school. Still, I was having a blast. And before I knew it, I was graduating and about to take my state boards to become a licensed hairstylist.

It took me seven shots to pass those boards. I struggled and struggled, but I had a good feeling about this and I didn't give up. What I discovered was that I needed to learn how to study. When I did, I passed the first time. Interesting what a little studying and practicing can do for you. Something as simple as those two skills may have changed my whole life if I had learned them earlier.

I was really proud that I had passed the boards, but it didn't necessarily mean I was a great hairstylist yet. I guessed it wasn't unusual to be less than confident when starting a new career. I've heard it said that you get your license from school but you get your education on the job. I was really looking forward to getting better since I had only mastered about two haircuts.

I was pretty excited to get my first real hairstyling job at a salon called NY Clippers in Schenectady. My first day, a client was sitting in my chair and told me she wanted layers. I didn't know how to cut layers, so I went up to the lady that managed the place and asked her how to do the cut. I thought her eyes were going to bug out of her head. But she explained how to do it in detail and I went back and I cut layers. I thought I did a pretty good job. (Hope you liked it — if not, I'm really sorry!)

After work, we'd go out partying and Sonny loved to announce loudly to everyone within earshot that I was a beautician and he still wasn't sure if I was gay or not. Of course, he would then retract it, but he really wasn't helping my self-esteem issues.

Even though I felt like a loser, it didn't stop me from taking risks, especially when we were out partying. I became known as the guy who would try anything. Maybe it was because I felt so insecure that I did that, but the rush of attention that I received quelled that lack of confidence in me, if only for a minute.

I also felt pretty good about some things at work, too, although my overall feeling was one of incompetence. I was able to keep clients (if they happened to like layered haircuts) for a fairly long time. The owners of NY Clippers mentored me and appreciated my skill at retailing. I really enjoyed helping people, and I was great at sales. As Vin had always told me, I was a real people person.

Vin said, "Giulio, you are fantastic at sales. You had a paper route that started as 50 customers, and you turned it into 300." He was right. I still have the "Top Newspaper Sales Route" trophy from the *Schenectady Gazette* on my desk.

I was good at sales at the salon. My clients left with everything they needed to recreate their hairstyles — products, blow dryers, curling irons, you name it.

I kept waiting for the magical moment to occur — that mystical experience that concluded with me becoming a master at cutting hair. I worked at NY Clippers for a year and it never really happened. I never got good at more than two or three haircuts.

I never saw huge waiting lists for my services. I never really did feel like I knew what I was doing. I never felt good at my job. I felt like every day presented a new challenge to get through it. I was getting bored.

I started to become dissatisfied with my career choice and wondered if I should look around and see what else was out there. I wondered what I was missing. I was still living at home, which made dating interesting to say the least, and I was getting restless in all areas of my life. I needed a change. Maybe I should start in the dating realm of my life. That seemed the easiest to control.

Your best decisions in life will come from your greatest experiences. Great experiences come from your greatest failures.

12.

Not A 20-Year-Old Virgin

Like I said, dating was a challenge since I was still living at home. It was a given that nobody really was able to live up to the Sunday night dinner expectations of the Veglio family. Anyone who knows Italian families know that the bonds are strong and must never be broken.

And nobody was ever going to be good enough. This was pretty intimidating for anyone outside of our family, of course, so I spent as much time outside our house as possible. Moving out would be unacceptable. You don't break tradition. You don't move away from family.

But I still had needs, you know? Even though I was an adult, since I was living at home, I had a curfew. Hey, that's just how things were, so it was useless to fight it.

Sonny showed me the easiest way to sneak out of the house. I climbed out my bedroom window, along the porch rooftop. It was pretty steep, and I had to be extremely quiet. My mother had ears like Superman. I crawled along the roof line until I found the right spot where I could hang until I felt the top of the fence. I caught my toe on the top of the fence and jumped over, landing on the neighbor's soft grass. I felt like I was 12, for Pete's sake.

One time my mother wasn't able to sleep. That was unusual for her. Usually, once she went to bed she was out for the night, but this time she was not only awake, but happened to be looking out the front window as I was climbing from the fence to the rooftop.

She waited in my room until I poked my head in the window, then grabbed a good chunk of my hair to "help" me in. Good thing my dad was a heavy sleeper, or he would have bolted up to my room and thrown me out the window with the force of a bull. This is when I would have definitely settled for a slap on the back of the head. It was as embarrassing as if a crowd had been watching the whole thing. The paranoia of worrying about that stuff!

One night at a club, I met a little beauty named Cindy. We really seemed to click. Vin and Sonny both thought she was really cute, too. I asked her out for a date that next Friday, and I pretty much decided to date her exclusively after that. She was good to me, had a great job, and was easy to talk to. We got along really well.

We had been dating a few weeks when St. Patrick's Day rolled around. We had been partying all night and feeling pretty good. Vin was even teasing me about how we couldn't keep our hands off each other at the club.

Cindy leaned over to me and seductively whispered, "let's go to my place."

I couldn't get out of my chair fast enough. We went back to her house and things heated up pretty quickly. We were ripping off each other's clothes so fast, they seemed to blur past me. It was like a scene from a movie. In the chaos of the moment, though, I caught a glimpse of her alarm clock next to the bed. It was nearly my curfew, and I was not going to make it home on time.

My libido screeched to a halt and so did hers when I sadly looked at her and said, "hold on a sec. I have to call my house and let my mom know I won't be home."

She sat straight up in bed with a disgusted look on her face. "What? You've gotta be kidding me."

"I wish I was," I said, miserably. "I wish I was."

That moment really changed our relationship. Cindy was seriously freaked out about my utter lack of independence at my age. She just wasn't sure she wanted to be involved with someone who was unable to be what she considered an adult. She was so angry with me she sent me packing right then and there.

I was telling Vin and Sonny about it the next night over a beer after work. Vin just shook his head and Sonny wouldn't shut up about how I was a mama's boy.

"Hey, mama's boy, your turn to buy the next round," he would shout. I was sure everyone in the bar could hear.

"Look," I said. "I mean, if someone wants to be a part of my life, but she won't respect my family the way they are, well then maybe I shouldn't worry about her, you know what I mean?"

Of course Vin understood, but Sonny just called me a wimp.

I left the bar that night, sad, a little defeated maybe. But I also knew that's how it had to be, at least for now. I had a feeling that this was all very temporary — that there were big changes just around the corner.

So maybe dating wasn't the most controllable area to change right now, after all. Maybe I should find a new salon to work in to give me a new working environment and new perspective on life.

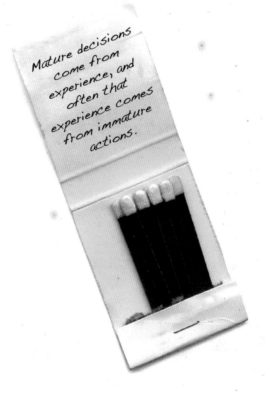

Mature decisions come from experience, and often that experience comes from immature actions.

13.

Finding My Way To The Perfect Life

There was a hot new salon in a mall just outside of Schenectady called Command Performance where I landed a job. Their advertising jingle was known across the nation. It went something like: *Command Performance, where you keep on looking like you looked when you left.* It seemed like an incredibly progressive and exciting place to work and I really enjoyed it.

I was getting better at hairstyling all the time and was beginning to perfect the big poofy hair that was so popular in the 80s. I was also doing a great job of selling products and other services. My sales skills were better than ever and my hairstyling was improving every day. I had developed a fairly loyal clientele and things were good.

While I was working at Command Performance, I had the opportunity to attend numerous hairstyling events and shows, which really helped me to refine my hairstyling ability. But the best part was that I got to see and meet respected professionals in the hairstyling industry. One of them was Paul Mitchell, who was on his way to celebrity status in the industry due to a handful of popular hair care products.

It was one of his first events in America. There was a small audience, around 30 people or so, and it really felt special. It was inspirational to meet the man who is now world renowned for his hair styling talents, and who's had so much success in America. The word that most comes to mind when I think of this event is "enthusiasm." The positive energy that rippled through the event was unforgettable. I remember being on the edge of my seat thinking, "I could do this! I'm like him."

I felt that I had a personality that would be great on stage. I had loved performing back in junior high school and I always loved being the center of attention. My family used to tell me I was a born performer.

Could this be a way that I could marry my love of the hair industry with my abilities as a performer? I saw possibilities and it motivated me to learn everything I could so one day I could be up there sharing my knowledge and enthusiasm with others who were as unsure of themselves as I often was.

Another person I met during this time was Sam Brocato, a highly regarded hair industry pro. He was known for his passion for creative design and product performance and spoke at trade shows and trainings that I attended. I was in awe of what he'd accomplished. What stood out was his confession of being a troublemaker like me, and a bad student to boot! He opened his first salon in 1976, with three more to follow. Here was another guy I could relate to, with a bit of a checkered past. He was successful, famous, talented and sharing all that with the world.

Although I had this new goal and motivation in my life, I felt that familiar unrest again. A salon owner I knew named David recruited me from Command Performance. He seemed very successful and I wanted what he had. I wanted to own my own business, so I went to see what I could learn from him.

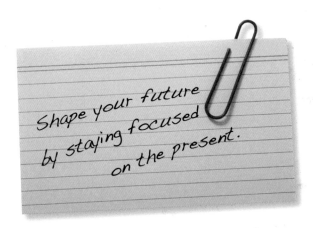

Shape your future by staying focused on the present.

14.
Like A Kid In
A Candy Store

I had been working at David's salon for a few months. I worked hard. I wanted to be just like him: have his success, his charisma, his confidence. I wanted his paycheck. I was constantly asking questions and trying to learn as much as possible from him. I sat down in one of the empty chairs and exhaled deeply as David sat down next to me.

The pace, the excitement and the joy of finding something that completely drew me in was taking its toll emotionally. It was all good. I was pumped but I was tired.

"Long week, Giulio?" He asked.

"Yeah, but I love it," I replied.

"You sure know how to work. I wonder if you know to relax. Maybe I should take you with me tonight and show you how."

I really admired David. He seemed to have everything I wanted. He owned his own business, was very successful at it, had girls and money. He lived the VIP lifestyle. When he went out, it was either in a limo or in his gorgeous new sports car.

"Sure," I said, mildly wondering what I was getting myself into. Whatever it was, I was sure it would be glamorous if it was with David.

"Great, it's going to be a good night," David said with a mischievous glint in his eye.

That look told me that he knew more about the evening's agenda than he wanted to disclose in that moment. This only made me more eager to spend time with David.

David and I pulled up to the glitzy, flashy place in his new, sleek sports car. We checked our hair, unbuttoned our collars and walked through the doors of David's favorite strip club. David entered like he owned the place. He directed us up front and center, took a seat and readied himself for the show. I plunked down in the seat to the left of him, as several girls flocked to his right.

Cocktails magically and immediately appeared and David raised his in a toast toward me.

"To new friends," he half shouted.

"To new friends," I toasted. We dove into our first drink, one of many that we would indulge in that night.

The drinks kept arriving. Girl after girl made her way onto the stage in front of us to perform her signature dance. Dollar after dollar was thrown, tucked and collected in very appropriate places.

It didn't take long to notice how most of the

ladies looked very familiar to me. Despite the alcohol I realized that almost every dancer was a client of David's. With that awareness I also remember feeling myself getting drowsy. At some point I checked my watch and was astounded to see two o'clock ticking away on my wrist.

I tapped David on the shoulder and pulled his attention away from the stage.

"Hey man, I think I'm going to call it a night," I slurred. I was wasted.

"What, Giulio? Things are just about to get better. Come on, follow me." David pushed back from his seat and disappeared behind the curtain that protected a black hallway from view.

We made our way down a smoky, cramped hallway into the dressing room area.

"This is the way to join the after-party," David offered as we emerged into the light of the back room. He had one scantily clad female draped on each arm.

I plopped down between two sets of fishnet stocking legs that were attached to women reclining on cushy chairs. David and his girls gathered on a sofa across from us with a coffee table in between.

"Giulio, your life is about to have a taste of some sweet, sweet shit."

David moved to the table while one of the women flanking him pulled a mirror off the wall and laid it in the center of the table. David took out a small glass vile and poured four lines of white powder on the mirror. Then he carefully removed a $100 bill from his wallet, rolled it up into a stubby yet tight straw and pointed it toward me.

"This is sweet nose candy, my man." Putting one end of the bill to his nose he traced the other end along a line of cocaine and effortlessly inhaled the entire thing.

My eyes blinked. My brain was trying to comprehend what I had just witnessed. By the growing look of satisfaction on David's face I knew he wanted us to follow his lead.

My gut twisted. I knew this was wrong and I heard Vin's voice saying, "don't do it, Giulio. Don't do it."

Sonny jumped up from the couch startling the ladies near his side. "How'd you do that?" he asked.

One of David's girls took the rolled bill from his grip and with a flirtatious movement or two placed it in Sonny's. Seductively she bent his head toward her lips and then to the table.

"Just breathe in baby," she said. "Suck it up smooth and easy now."

Sonny was a natural. He made it look as easy as David had. A thin film of sweat was beginning to bead up on David's forehead. His eyes had widened and as I looked back at Sonny the same thing was happening to him.

Another woman took the straw and moved herself into my lap. "Your turn Mister Giulio," she enticed. My hand reached for the bill.

I looked at Sonny. "Do it man," he said. "You've got to try this shit."

I could hear the logic in me screaming to get up and leave. I could hear my parents' voices in the back of my head asking me what I was thinking. A battle in my conscious was waging. Why would David, my new mentor, do anything to hurt me? Why would one of my best friends, Sonny, hurt me?

I looked at the two remaining lines of cocaine. This was the first time I had ever seen it. Without a word I lifted the bill to my right nostril.

Wow! It took me from sleepy to being wide awake. From blah to ALIVE! In the moment, it made everything amazing. I was perfect. Life was perfect. Everything was perfect. I had more confidence and wonderfulness than I knew what to do with.

As I look back on this day now, I wonder if I'd been more confident, more sure of myself, if I'd have had the wherewithal to say "no." I wonder how many people, every day, make bad choices because they don't feel good enough about themselves to say "no." I would wager that the number has to be huge.

I've seen magazine articles in the salon that point to the fact that many of us hear and believe we are not good enough. That's where drugs make an impact. They make us feel like we can do anything, be anything.

Drugs make you feel "more than" instead of "less than." They make it so you don't ever want to NOT do them. The power of the drugs holds you firmly until it eventually kills you, or you experience the wretched but blessed release.

Self deceit turns the truth into a cycle of lies.

MICHELOB
BEER

15.
The Life Of The Party

The next day, I felt numb and I kind of avoided David. I think I was overwhelmed by what had happened last night and the easiest way to deal was to not think or talk about it at all.

The trouble was I LOVED the way coke made me feel. Even more troubling was that I wanted that feeling all the time now. I couldn't stop thinking about it, no matter how hard I tried not to. In fact, the opposite was true. The more I tried NOT to think about it, the more I DID think about it.

That night, I went to a party at a friend's house. I was very tired from working all day and I had fallen into a rut, so I had decided I was going to try cocaine again. For the first time in a long time I had felt light, happy and hopeful.

I decided to ask David how to get some more the next day at work. At the party I was unusually quiet. I just felt like fading into the background that night. Since I normally like to be the life of the party, this was unusual for me.

I sat on the end of a sofa in a back room, drinking beer after beer after beer. I could still hear all the music and laughter but I was alone with my thoughts. A cute, bubbly girl who I'd seen at lots of parties but never officially met before bopped over to me and plunked herself down on the sofa next to me. She grinned at me and I couldn't help but smile back.

She looked at me as if memorizing my face. I stared back, although a bit more quizzically.

"You know what you need?" She asked me.

"What," I wondered

"You need a little pick-me-up." She smiled even wider. "You need a touch of something sweet."

Well of course she was right, I remember thinking. My face and the big bags under my eyes were a dead giveaway, even if my expression tried very hard to belie the underlying exhaustion. Even the mass quantities of beer I had been consuming hadn't numbed me quite enough. That IS what I need. Over her left shoulder I caught a glimpse of Sonny, who was nodding approvingly.

She had piqued my curiosity and I watched her attentively as she opened up her purse and extracted a mirror and a small packet. From the packet she removed a razor blade, and proceeded to sprinkle a bit of the powder on the mirror. I was mesmerized as she skillfully used the razor blade to create thin lines of powder on the mirror. She then proceeded to sniff it hard through her nostril using a rolled-up dollar bill.

I couldn't believe my luck.

I mean, I had just been sitting there thinking about the stuff and she appeared!

"Your turn," she pronounced. She proceeded to sprinkle out another bit of powder and skillfully scrape it into a line.

"You ever try this before?"

I looked at her blankly as I nodded my head and said, "once."

I've heard it said that if you try it once and never do it again, you've experimented. But if you go back for seconds, you're done for. As of that moment, I was done for.

After that, my whole life consisted of this routine: work, girls, party all night until the bars closed or they kicked us out, go to someone's house and party some more until it was time to shower and get ready for work again. I don't think I slept more than a couple of hours a night. I'd drink coffee, but I was still tired so I'd hit some coke to keep me going.

I was living the life using VIP rooms at every bar, limos, even a pager so I could screen calls and only talk to who I wanted to. David showed me how to make the most money by working like crazy, then playing like crazy.

I was still living at home with no expenses to speak of, so all my money went to my lifestyle and to my habit. To every onlooker, it would seem that I had everything going for me — women, worth, money. But it was all a façade.

David was starting to really lose it. His coke use was getting in the way of his business big time. He would go for days and not come into work, sometimes calling to arrange for me to take his clients, but it was getting old fast.

To top it off, he stopped paying me, and that was about it. I started looking for another place to hang my hat.

My dream of owning my own salon hadn't died. I knew it was just a matter of time before that dream became a reality. I was still unsure of how it would actually come about or when, but I remained optimistic.

Little did I know that my father was even more confident. He wasn't too thrilled about me being a hairstylist, but me owning my own business was as important to him as it was to me.

In our town, there was an area we called "Hairdresser's Alley" because every other house or shop was a salon. It was here on one of my dad's walks that he met a guy who was offering his salon for rent. It was small — just four chairs — but it was available for only $300 a month. My father jumped at it the minute he saw it. Out of the blue, he surprised me with the lease.

At the age of 21, I was now a business owner. And I was excited!

Of course, Sonny did his best to squelch my new interest. Vin and my family were supportive so I was eager to show them I could do it. I felt young and inexperienced in business, but I knew this was a step I needed to take.

Giulio's Hair Design, which I later changed to Giulio's International Hair Design, was born. It was small, but we were busy almost immediately. The location was just around the corner from David's, so I had lots of my previous clients follow me. I built up my clientele and added employees, until we were at capacity, and had waiting lists galore. I was finally hitting my stride and I loved every minute.

Time flew by, and before I knew it, we were celebrating our first anniversary at the salon and the second was soon to come.

I was making some really serious money with my salon but my love of cocaine overshadowed everything I did, including my business. I continued to party when I left work.

One night when I was out with friends, they urged me to get up on stage for an open mic comedy performance.

"You're funny," they all said. "Get up there!" I hesitated at first, but then I thought "what the hell" and went on stage. I was surprised when I rocked the house!

I started performing more regularly, and even worked some of the larger clubs like the Tropicana in Atlantic City. But coke directed my life. It didn't help that it was prevalent backstage at the clubs. Other performers and club owners alike were constantly doing cocaine and it flowed freely. Although I was really enjoying entertaining, it wasn't surprising when cocaine got in the way of that dream. Eventually, IT wins, and everything else just falls away. I just stopped showing up.

On the surface everything was hunky dory, but I was sinking more and more into a deep depression. I was getting behind at work, dropping the ball on things that should have been second nature. I started lying about even the stupidest things. I got really good at lying, or so I thought. I wonder now if I was really fooling anyone.

More seriously, there were days when I thought I was going to die. My heart would just start racing for no reason. I wasn't sleeping, so I'd drink coffee to try and wake up, but it only made me more tired and depressed.

So I'd do a bit more coke, then I'd feel so awake even though I was tired. But I was always so high that I never slept. I'd get depressed again, and the only thing that seemed to bring me out of the depression was coke. So I'd do some more, then get more depressed as I came down a bit, and well, you get the picture. It was a vicious cycle.

Add some really unhealthy extreme paranoia — and the fact that I was totally broke — to that picture and you see that I was one messed up guy. I came to mistrust my friends and my coworkers. In fact, I became mistrustful of everyone around me.

I was spending all my money — all my tips, paycheck, everything — on cocaine. I made it last as long as I could, but it seemed to disappear faster and faster every time I'd get some more.

Before too long, I began cutting and selling cocaine, too. Obviously, I wasn't a big-time dealer. I really only made enough to support my habit, but I didn't care. Frankly that was the most important thing in my life. Every little bit I'd get extra went to buy more blow.

I even lost my girlfriend at the time because I had one moment of honesty where I told her that I cared more for cocaine than I did about her. I pick the damnedest times to be honest. I did crave love and passion. I went through lots and lots of girls but my strongest allegiance was to my real love: cocaine.

Things were going downhill really fast. I lost my best girl. I lost my sports car. My clients were dropping like flies, and creditors were calling constantly. My health was certainly suffering, but frankly, that was the least of my concerns.

If I just kept my high going, I felt like Superman! It was like I was infallible and could conquer the world! That's what the shit does to you. You are so numb you don't realize that your world is falling apart, and you wouldn't care if you did know.

It's interesting how I remember watching coke control David's life when I was working in his salon. I felt such disdain for him. I even asked myself, "why can't he get hold of his problem?" Now I realize it's because he didn't see it, just like I didn't see it in my own life.

The proverbial "rock bottom" was looming dangerously

close, but I was oblivious. The cocaine kept my denial suspended just above the bottom level of hell. It was hot, but not yet scorching. Real hell was just around the corner.

My friends had changed, too, of course. I never saw Vin. I just didn't seem to fit into his life anymore.

One Saturday at the salon, Sonny showed up with some other friends.

"Hey, loser, I haven't seen you in forever. Let's hang out tonight. There's a party over at Flanagan's. Wanna go?"

"Yeah, but my car, uh, isn't working right now. Pick me up around eight and we'll go."

"Awesome. See ya then."

What a crazy night at Flanagan's! Sonny and I found a couple of pretty girls who were going to someone's house with a bunch of people, so we happily accompanied them. Booze, coke, pot, whatever you wanted was readily available at every turn in this house. It was nuts, but fun! The whole thing was kind of a fog. Time flew by, and people started falling asleep wherever they could find a square foot of floor, sofa, bed, whatever. There were people in the bathtub, even.

The girls and I had stayed away from the pot and just concentrated on the coke and booze all night, so we weren't tired. We just stayed up in one of the bedrooms we had found earlier and locked the door. We made out, we talked, we snorted coke for hours and hours.

I must have fallen asleep for a minute, because I remember being startled awake with a nagging sensation that I was supposed to be doing something important. I looked outside the window and it looked like dusk.

I was totally disoriented. Where was I? How did I get here? Who is this girl? Where am I supposed to be? What day is it? Did I really party and sleep away a whole day?

I saw a telephone on the nightstand and dialed the number for the time. It was 6:00 pm. Okay. It was Tuesday. Okay. TUESDAY? Shit. Oh, well, so I missed another day of work. I hoped my few appointments got rescheduled or taken care of. Not that I really cared a lot.

I started getting dressed, trying desperately to remember the significance of the day. I couldn't find anyone I knew. I just let the girl, whoever she was, sleep. I guessed she could find her own way home.

I stepped over people, making my way to the front door, when another guy I know from the party scene emerged from the kitchen with Sonny.

"Hey," said Joe. "Let's go to my house and clean up a bit — maybe have a bite to eat. I'm just down the street."

"Sounds good," I said. "I need a shower."

"Yeah, you can take one at my house."

"Cool, let's go."

As we made our way to Joe's house, I was still plagued by the feeling I was forgetting something. "Oh, well," I thought. "It will come to me."

At Joe's there were a few people hanging out, so after I showered, I decided to stay for a bit. They had some coke and were willing to share. The one thing I never turned down was free cocaine, so I stayed and partied a while longer. Besides, I had already blown off the day, why not a few more hours?

That moment began the longest drug binge I had ever been on. Hours turned into days. They all ran together and I never went outside. In fact, I barely left the sofa. I may have slept some. I may have eaten some. I can't really be sure. I don't even know how many days I stayed at Joe's house. People came in and out and I just stayed and stayed and stayed. Nobody seemed to mind or even notice I was there, really.

I would float in and out of my high, crash, sleep a bit, wake up, get high again, lather, rinse and repeat. I didn't care about anything or anyone. All I cared about was that we didn't run out of coke.

The coming down parts were harsh. That's when the cocaine started to wear off and the mess that I'd become started to stare me in the face. I was so riddled with guilt and felt so crappy that the only thing I wanted to do was to get high again, because that's the only time I felt good. I was beginning to hate myself.

I was in and out of this feeling of failure and regret. I was starting to realize that I couldn't handle NOT being high, and that scared the shit out of me. But that didn't last for long, as I'd snort another line and forget.

I realized that this had become a pattern for me — not just during this crazy, extended binge, but in the past, too. I was losing control. I no longer had the wherewithal to say no, not even to myself.

I needed help, but I didn't know how or who to ask. And I was ashamed.

So, in my confusion, I chose getting high again. That's what I always chose when I was unsettled. It was amazing how coke made me feel like I had nothing to worry about.

The next day, I was watching cartoons on TV, sitting on the sofa in a stupor when someone knocked on the door. I didn't even glance up when my sister, Elvira and her husband, Glenn, came in and sat by me on the sofa. They were furious yet worried and relieved all at once. Elvira didn't know whether to hug me or shake me or slap me or kiss me. So she did all of it, almost at once.

"You look like shit," Glenn said. I looked at him with vacant eyes. I probably did.

"You missed Father's Day!" My sister screamed at me.

I said nothing when it hit me. It was Father's Day! I had missed Father's Day! Of all days! Crap.

We always had a huge family dinner at noon time to celebrate important days and I had completely missed what has always been an important day in my family's life. How was I going to explain that one?

Turns out my family had been searching for me for days. When I missed Father's Day, they knew something was drastically wrong. I had been a flake, true, and had missed things recently that I'd never have missed in the past, but this was an event that you just didn't ditch in my family, and they knew I was in trouble.

They began by asking all my friends and then went to the salon, where one of my employees gave them a couple of ideas. They'd been concerned, too, since I hadn't been at work, but they were really more pissed than worried like my family was. I can understand how they felt, since I felt the same way with David's frequent disappearances.

A girl who was getting her hair done at the salon happened to overhear the questioning, and she had also happened to be at Flanagan's for the party that night. She led them to some other people who thought I might be at Joe's, since he kind of had a "slam pad" — the place where people just showed up to party and sleep until they left.

After days of partying, I wasn't in the best of shape. They helped me up and we stumbled down the stairs together and out to their car. I went obligingly, but I was so weak.

"Where are you taking me?" I asked.

My sister sounded disgusted when she said, "we're

taking you to our house to clean you up and then we are taking you home to mom and dad."

Dad. The mere thought of dad and how I had missed Father's Day caused the rock in my gut to grow a bit. I knew it was time to have a long talk with my parents and confess, but I sure didn't want to. What would they think? What would they do?

My dad was going to kill me, I thought miserably. I just really didn't want to disappoint them. But there was a tiny, tiny part of me that was light inside. I think there was a little inkling that maybe this was my way out of the downward spiral I was on.

By the time we were on the way to my parents' house, I had nothing but images of their faces in my head.

"I am in serious need of a hit," I thought to myself. Then I shook my head. What was I thinking? Here I am, en route to my parents' house to break their hearts and all I can think of is myself?

"I am a selfish asshole," I berated myself all the way there. When we pulled up in front of their house, I could barely move out of the car. It was like my butt was cemented to the seat. I was so dreading this.

I thought of how my father would react. My father had given up everything he knew and everything he owned so that we could have opportunities to succeed like we never would have in Italy. I suddenly realized that my actions were a virtual slap in his face.

Of course, I hadn't meant for it to go this far. Nobody ever does. Nobody ever sets out to become addicted. That's the part we think we can trick. We think, "what the hell, one more time won't hurt me. It doesn't mean I'm ADDICTED or anything. I can quit anytime I want."

That's the denial that had kept me going all this time. I mean, you don't have to quit if it hasn't become a problem, right? But drug use is like a slippery snake, slowly coiling its way up your body, wrapping itself around and around until it has a firm hold on your neck, then it squeezes, and squeezes, progressively tighter, until one day you either fight it, stab it, shoot it, throw it off, finally recognizing the threat, or you allow yourself to succumb to the certain death it offers.

Here was the first stage of my fight. As I forced myself out of the car and toward the steps of my parents' house, I felt like I was walking through mud. Every step was an effort. My mother was at the front door, her face a contorted demonstration of the worry and fear I had caused her. My heart twisted with grief for what I had done.

She followed us into the front room, where my father was sitting in his favorite chair, staring out the window. As he turned to look at me, I suddenly realized that he wasn't a young man anymore. When had those wrinkles around his eyes become so pronounced? I knew that what I had to tell him today would age him even more. I had a pit in my stomach the size of a football.

Then, I sat down, faced my parents, who loved me far more than I deserved, especially at that moment, and I broke their hearts. I said the hardest words I had ever said.

"Mom, dad, I have a drug problem."

The words hung in the air, as if they didn't know where to fall. Nobody said anything for what seemed like forever.

My mother nodded, tears streaming down her face. Dad was composed, but the hurt was written in his eyes. They were so quiet I wondered if they had already known. I guess they had probably suspected as much, with my erratic behavior and disappearances. But to actually say the words, and admit out loud that I did have a drug problem, was surprisingly liberating. I know that they — especially my mother — were primarily concerned with me, but also with other people might think.

I felt like crap for hurting my parents and my family the way I had, but there was a certain freeing feeling about having said the words, like maybe it was more of a beginning than an ending.

We talked about what to do and my parents insisted that I go to Italy. I would be far enough away from the habits I had established here, and I could clean myself up and get back on my feet. My older brother, Giuseppe, was in medical school in Milan, and I could live with him.

For the next week, I dried out at my parent's house, and then I boarded the plane to Italy, where I could have a new lease on life.

The irony of it struck me as the plane ascended above New York's skyline. We came to America for the new opportunities, and I had to go back to Italy to find them. It's ironic how things turn out sometimes.

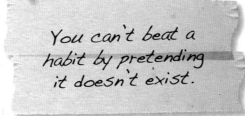

You can't beat a habit by pretending it doesn't exist.

16.
Bella Italia

As I got acquainted with Giuseppe's place and life in Italy, I realized that hair in Milan was entirely different than hair in New York. Women and men alike in America sported big, poofy 1980s styles, and I had become good at creating that look. So good, in fact, that I was "unconsciously competent." I didn't even have to think about how to do it, I just did it. Well, as beneficial as that could be in America, it wasn't helpful in Italy. Styles there were long and straight.

I went on numerous tryouts and wasn't hired at any of them. Even the sinks were different in Europe — they were stand-behind sinks, while I was used to the American side-stance. The first time I washed someone's hair, the hose was completely out of control and I totally soaked the poor woman.

The salon owner rushed over, yelling *"Basta! Basta! Basta!"* "Enough! Stop! That will do."

My brother had made some inquiries and he helped me find a job doing hair. He talked with a salon owner and told her that I'd owned a salon in the past, so she reasoned that I must be good. After my third blow-dry, she paid me in advance for the next month and her face told me to get the hell out.

After the humiliation of not even being able to do hair, the only job I'd ever known, combined with the humiliation of hitting rock bottom at home and coming out here in the first place, the decision to go back to beauty school wasn't that hard.

Getting to school was a journey in itself. In Europe, people walk everywhere. This didn't hurt my physique at all, but it took some getting used to. There was the subway, but it stopped about two miles short of the beauty school I was attending at night. After a subway ride, I would get off and walk the rest of the way, two miles, to get to the school.

It made me nervous because I had to walk by what we would consider a "red light district." I didn't know if I was supposed to greet or acknowledge the prostitutes, or just not look at them. I jammed my hands in my pockets and forged my way through very quickly. Every now and again, I would glance up and say "hi," but it made me really uncomfortable, especially when I suspected that some of those pretty girls were actually guys.

After a while, though, I got used to them. I even got to know some of those prostitutes (not what you're thinking!). Sometimes all it takes is a "hello" to find out that people can really be nice.

Centro Stilo Moda, the combination school and salon that I attended and worked in was, the first place where I really understood hair. I had cut, styled, perm-ed, and blow-dried hair for all this time, but never really GOT it. Now, I was finally getting it, understanding how hair moves and behaves and how to work with it, rather than force it into what I wanted it to do.

I got to where I could wrap perms with my eyes closed. I was also trying to earn as much money as I could, because my mother had bailed me out of my debts and messes and drug-related issues at home with $10,000 of her hard-earned savings. I had to pay her back as quickly as possible. I wanted to show her and my father that they could still be proud of me one day.

I did have a social life, too. I would go to bars and talk instead of drink. It was strange at first, not getting wasted every time I walked into a bar, but I liked it. I actually got to know people.

I thought a lot about returning home, but I was afraid to. Every time I even thought about it, I felt a little sense of panic grip my stomach. I wasn't ready yet. What if I went back and got back into coke? I wasn't certain of my strength to resist it. I had to gain more confidence first.

I also believe that I still had much to learn. Looking back on my life in Italy, I know that it was a turning point in my career. I think it started with me being humbled by hitting rock bottom. That experience opened me up for new understandings — not just about life in general, but about hair.

One of the school's owners, Jean-Michel, for reasons unbeknownst to me, took a liking to me. I don't know why, but he really took me under his wing and showed me the ropes. He was hard on me, flicking me with his comb with a disapproving glance every time I did something wrong or questioned something he said.

I'll never forget the first time I watched Jean-Michel cut someone's hair. It was like an art form, like an amazing blur of creative artistry. It was a lady with long blond hair and he turned her upside down and went at her with two pairs of scissors like Edward Scissorhands. I was enthralled.

Jean-Michel took time with me, like a father would take time with his son, passing on a legacy. He told me to "stop mimicking haircuts and start understanding them." I was fairly certain he didn't know what the hell he was talking about, but I did my best to do everything he said, since he was very well-respected in the city and throughout the industry.

I respected him, too. I begged to work at his salon during the day. I was willing to sweep hair, restock product, what ever I could do, for no pay. I was so eager to learn and just absorb all of Jean-Michel's knowledge and his talent as possible.

I'm not sure why he allowed me to hang around the way I did. I'm sure I was a nuisance sometimes, but he believed in me. Finally, someone believed in me. He chose me. He wanted to teach me the "whys" of the "how." His own staff didn't receive the attention that Jean-Michel gave me. I had the advantage of having his assistance all day at the salon and all night at school.

I was reminded of my excitement a few years back when I met Paul Mitchell and Sam Brocato and how determined I was to go down that path of teaching and motivating others. Meeting them created a stream of "aha!" moments that, combined with my association with my friend and mentor, Jean-Michel, really helped me define my career. When I thought about how I wanted to give back when I returned to America, I thought of these men who had influenced my professional life.

That's what I wanted to do.

My self-esteem had started to shift while I was in Italy. It wasn't just Jean-Michel and that association. Everyone was different here — very encouraging, like a group of personal coaches. They were all about building the ego, which is exactly

what I needed. Even my brother never even mentioned my faults and past mistakes. It was as if they'd never happened. Everywhere I went I was uplifted and met with support.

Maybe it is because of the extreme beauty there. Everything is beautiful in Italy — the people, the country, the food, the wine, the lifestyle. There was no judgment. Or was it just because I was looking at life through new eyes?

There were drugs available, of course. It was Milan, the Mecca of the fashion and modeling industry. It wasn't unusual to be walking down the street and see a car pull up to someone standing on the corner. The bystander would reach his cash-filled fist into the window, receive his hit with a much-used needle, and the car would speed off. So would the bystander.

I saw others who lived that drug-filled lifestyle and I didn't want it. It was a lifestyle that included prostitutes, people sleeping in alleys, jail, lives ruined. I saw people die because of drugs.

It's just that I felt so good. I was high on life and didn't need drugs to make me feel good. I found my self-esteem. I felt great and I looked great. Walking everywhere and eating the down to-earth foods that Italians enjoy improved my appearance from the inside out.

I had fallen in love with Italy. Everything about living there made me feel good, except that my family back in America was getting quite anxious for me to return.

My sister, Elvira, had agreed to manage my salon while I was gone. My family had gone to great lengths to make sure that our family name was protected and that my mistakes wouldn't cause them embarrassment. This included making sure my business stayed open in my absence. But it was faltering big time, and I was expected to give it a boost again.

My father summoned me to return. And, though I dearly wanted to stay, I was ready to show everyone how I had changed during my year in Italy. With all my parents had done and spent to keep up appearances, I knew deep down that it just wasn't possible to stay right now.

My journey down the path of cocaine made me stronger. I guess I had to overcome cocaine to know that I was capable of overcoming many things. It's not a path I would ever recommend. I'm one of the fortunate ones who survived. Survive I did, and that's when my life really seemed to begin. But I wasn't in the clear quite yet.

A return to your roots often helps you understand where you're going.

Part Four

Change Is A
State Of Mind

rhythm of success

Self-Made
in America
by John McCormack

17.

Arriving At The Threshold

Although I knew I was in a much better place, both physically and mentally, I was still nervous about being back home in America. I felt fairly sure I could resist my previous drug-ridden lifestyle, but it was weird — like that was all I could remember doing when I lived there. It was hard to picture anything else.

I knew that the key to my survival would be to dive into my career and find others who were in need, so I could give back to them some of what I had learned and received from Jean-Michel.

I was sad that I'd had to let go of my relationships with people whom I had spent time with before I left for Italy, but I knew it was for the best. There were rumors that I was a narc, due to my disassociation from that life, but I'd expected some of that. I knew my truth, and that was all that mattered.

My mother has always quoted this statement to me: "Tell me who you hang with and I'll tell you who you are."

For the first time, I really understood what she meant by that. It gave me a whole new perspective on who I wanted to be. I was driving this bus, and I got to choose which direction it was headed. It was not headed to Cocaine Street. EVER!

Although Elvira had done her best to keep the salon afloat while I was gone, she unfortunately didn't have much to work with. The stylists I'd hired before I left to go to back to Italy were struggling with the same cocaine demons I was at that time, and one by one they had gone away.

In fact, when I returned in 1987, there was only one stylist working and she was someone my sister had hired. So, it was time for me to start over, and I did. I set out to rebuild, but this time, with a fresh attitude and renewed spirit.

I gravitated toward a younger crowd of new hairstylists. My intention was to become the mentor to them that Jean-Michel had been to me. He gave me a gift that I wanted to pass on, so I dove in headfirst. I also knew that anything I could do to stay busy would help to keep me away from what I didn't want to be doing: drugs.

Although I had confidence now that I didn't before, it felt like I had a thick shell around me. Inside, there was still some vulnerability, but I was determined to keep it safely enclosed in that shell. Still, I wavered sometimes. Could I keep the shell intact forever? Most days, I was sure that I could, but some days, doubts just had a way of creeping in.

There was a part of me that still craved the VIP, limo-riding Giulio that I was before going to Italy. I also kind of missed the adrenaline rush I experienced almost every day during that time. It was exciting being high all the time, living on the edge.

But I knew in my heart of hearts that it wasn't worth the price. I forced myself to remember the crap I had seen: heart attacks at such an early age, turning to prostitution to pay for the habit, lives wasting away in jail, people actually dying every day because of drugs. I had to keep focused on the real side of drug use.

Vin helped. He was my encouragement in America, my personal cheerleader. Sonny joined us sometimes, but he was still a goof off and I really wanted to separate myself from being a goof off. I wanted to move beyond that.

It's hard to think about moving anywhere fast when all you have to drive around is a bright red moped. Hey, it was at least transportation. The worst moments were when I pulled up at a stoplight with my little putt-putt whirring away, and a huge, badass Harley roared up next to me. I felt about three inches tall. I would just look straight ahead and think, "someday." Someday.

I was doing what I could to find my way back in New York. I wanted to be a mentor to younger hairstylists, but being broke I felt they had nothing to aspire to in me. I attended every event that I could, networking and trying to find a way to be something to somebody.

During one of these events, I had the opportunity to see Paul Mitchell again, and I recalled what an impression he had made on me in the past. His success had skyrocketed and seemed to know no limits. He had developed a very successful line of hair products and I very much admired both the products and the philosophy behind them.

That day, I called the distributor of Paul Mitchell's products and asked if I could be an educator. I told them I would sweep the floors or whatever I had to do to be part of what I considered to be a movement. I read the labels to educate myself and sold the product, which I liked very much. It was productive work and kept me busy.

I had a lot of fun with the other people on the show circuit. I still partied a bit — tequila slammers were the drink of the day - but I kept a lid on it for the most part. Control was key, and so far, I was doing okay. I won't say I was never tempted, old habits die hard. But I kept remembering what the end result might be if I went down that path again. Not for me, I told myself. Not for me.

I was looking for a new girlfriend, though — I always was. Some guys were crazy about cars, some crazy about clothes, whatever. Me, I was crazy about girls. I couldn't tell you the difference between a distributor cap and a piston, but I could tell you a fine looking booty when I saw one.

And one day at a show, I saw one. I was busy organizing product, getting ready for the event later that day, and I caught a glimpse of a beautiful young lady out of the corner of my eye. I about dropped all the bottles that were in my hand. That was seriously the finest butt I had seen in a while.

My eyes traveled up the body, around the curves and landed on a face that — wait! I knew that face!

"Laura!"

"Giulio!"

We yelled each other's names in unison and hugged. Laura's family and my family had known each other for years. I always knew she and her sisters would all grow up to be beautiful, but they seemed too young for me at the time. Besides, I was kind of known as the family "ladies man" and I always had a girlfriend.

I hadn't known she would be this pretty, though, and she seemed plenty grown up now! She had a great body, a great face and even great hair. She was gorgeous. We chatted for a few minutes, until I started getting looks from the rest of the event crew.

Before she walked away, I blurted, "we should go out!" To my surprise, she agreed and we made arrangements.

I could not stop thinking about her. The day we were supposed to go out, I was at the salon sweeping up after my last client. I was, of course, thinking of Laura and her killer booty.

That last client (I can't remember her name, but I do remember her huge chest) came up to me and boldly and suggestively asked what I was doing later that night. She made it pretty clear that if my plans included her, I was definitely getting some.

I thought about Laura. There was a certain respect that would be required there, and I knew sex was out of the question on my first date with her — Laura that is. Besides, both of our families knew we were planning a date (thanks to my cousin, who was doubling with us) and they were, of course, thrilled. Not only was she a nice Italian girl, but it was Laura — the nice Italian girl with the nice Italian booty!

Not that I minded the respect part of it — she was certainly worthy of my respect. But I was, well, horny. I considered not showing up to my date with Laura.

Later, over pizza, I told Vin and Sonny of my dilemma. Vin was horrified.

"Giulio, how could you even consider not going? I mean, you have done nothing but talk about Laura since you reconnected."

He had a point. I was fairly consumed by my thoughts of her.

Sonny had his two cents, though, too: "Screw that, man, you have a chance to get laid and you're gonna be bored with this date anyway."

Yes, another point to consider.

Vin countered with the clincher: "Giulio, you promised. You can't go back on your word."

Sonny pounded the table. "Listen, man, you can get in those pants tonight. Why would you pass up that opportunity?" That's all Sonny ever thought about.

I said, "listen, I'll show up. If things go well with Laura, I'll stay and hang out. If they don't, I'll call up the other girl and get me some of that." Thinking back, I can't believe I had such a male—chauvinistic attitude — especially toward my first date with a woman I was so crazy about.

Armed with my foolish contingency plan, my expectations for the night were minimal. Laura and I went to a club and started dancing. Boy, did we dance! I never gave another thought to big boobs girl again.

Laura and I seemed to fit together like two puzzle pieces. We moved. We grooved. Dancing is like having sex. It's more sensual sometimes than getting right down to business, if you know what I mean.

Did I really miss out on anything? Absolutely not. My life changed that night. Today, it makes me cringe to think about everything I would have missed out on had I skipped my date with Laura.

We never left the dance floor. After about five hours of dancing, we closed down the bar. But neither of us wanted the night to end. We hopped in my mom's blue Ford Escort, went to Denny's restaurant and talked nonstop into the morning. Laura was amazing — intelligent, beautiful and wise.

I found it hard to say goodbye for the night; I knew

I had to see her again — and soon. I asked her out again and she said yes. After three months of dating, we were engaged, and a year later, we were married. Our families were ecstatic.

Marriage has been interesting, to say the least. In the beginning, it was perfect. After that, it's work. I've learned to compromise and to choose my battles. Some things are just not worth fighting over. We also have both agreed that if there is a fight, and there will be fights, stay and work it out. Don't run to the bar. Clear the air and go to the same bed.

We've had some good times and we've had some bad times, but here we are, almost 20 years later, and we're still together, side by side. With all its ups and downs, it's worth it. Family is everything. Laura has supported and encouraged me in a way that I never expected anyone to do.

Life is a process where you always have the chance to change directions.

18.
Winn-Win Situations

I found that I needed support and encouragement fairly regularly. One of the most positive and optimistic people who came into my life was Winn Claybaugh. Now the dean and co-owner of Paul Mitchell Schools and a widely recognized hair and beauty industry leader, he welcomed me as a friend and colleague with open arms. And I needed that right about then.

My education in Italy established me in the industry as a good resource in the artistry of hairstyling. My mentor, Jean-Michel, influenced me to see that hairstyling was more than basic skills and going through the motions. It was important to feel what you are doing and to focus on your guest's needs. Note that I gave up using the term "client" since "guest" better describes the new attitude

114

I developed toward my customers. When you make these mental adjustments, hairstyling with emotion becomes an art.

I was asked to speak at an industry educational event in 1989 in New York City. As I prepared to go on stage, there was another guy there waiting his turn, and he looked pretty nervous. Winn Claybaugh was at the event to share his business success and know-how. I introduced myself and cracked a couple of jokes to ease his tension. We have been friends ever since. In fact, I count Winn as one of the most important people in my life.

Since his specialty was business productivity and motivation, and mine was creativity and artistry, we balanced each other very well. We completely enjoyed working together. His down-to-earth personality and encouragement were just what I needed, and I tried to made things fun for him.

We soon found ourselves booking event after event so we could each share the stage with someone that we really respected — one another. We also shared a mutual philosophy that our knowledge was important for the students and professionals in the industry.

In fact, Winn had a hairstyling school in Provo, Utah, where he invited me to come and work with his students. I did this on my own time and money because I enjoyed it so much. In return, Winn would come to New York and teach at my salon.

Winn was very supportive, and when I told him I was thinking about recording CDs that would highlight our focus on the value of enthusiastic, committed people in the hair industry, he was my biggest cheerleader. I wanted to share the message of believing in yourself. I had a lot to say about how anyone, no matter rich or poor, well-educated or street smart, can achieve a dream as long as he or she has a passion and vision to succeed.

My first CD set was called *Rhythm of Success*. It has touched the lives of many people and been very well received. Even today, event attendees seek me out after I've spoken to thank me for my CDs. They tell me that they've made a difference in their lives and given them hope for the future. They say that my CDs motivated them to go after their dreams.

This makes me feel incredibly good since my personal mission is to inspire and encourage others through my work.

I've had lots of experience in starting things with passion and little else. In 1993, I was in the middle of establishing a big salon in Clifton Park, New York. I didn't have much money, but I had dreams and I had bargaining abilities. Where there's a will, there's a way, right? Well, there was definitely a will.

This place was going to be 3,000 square feet and I was excited and scared as hell at the same time.

I had made friends with a contractor, Alfonso, and he was willing to work with me on the shoestring arrangements I could afford. I kept building my clientele as the construction went on around us. As I made money, I paid him. If I didn't make money, construction stopped and we worked in disarray until I could scrape together enough cash to move to the next project.

Why and how Alfonso stayed involved with me as long as he did, I don't know. But I'll never forget his patience.

There was a salesman that came around, as they always did, asking me to advertise in the local penny saver newspaper. Those guys sure are persistent!

This particular salesman was great at building relationships as part of the sales process and we would talk when we could. One day he said to me, "Giulio, I want you to read a book."

ME? Read a book! Ha! He didn't know who he was talking to! I'd never read a book in my life! I don't read! I'm just a stupid Italian kid who can barely speak English, much less READ it! Who is he kidding?

I told you he was persistent. He told me I must read *Self-Made in America* by John McCormack. I absolutely had to. He told me the nearest bookstore to my salon where I could find it, and I nodded politely and thanked him for the suggestion, never intending to take him up on it.

So it was to my great surprise that after work that night, I found myself in that bookstore. I found myself asking for *Self-Made in America* by John McCormack. And I found myself reading the back cover with interest.

My surprise heightened when I took the book home and actually started reading it!

In fact, I couldn't put it down. The story was amazing. McCormack describes his own experiences from working as a New York City policeman to becoming a Wall Street trader and entrepreneur. He made and lost his first million dollars before he was 25. It was then that he received invaluable counsel from a mentor.

This teacher and other entrepreneurs who advised McCormack were immigrants who through their intelligence, ingenuity, and diligence had achieved success. Eventually, McCormack and his wife Maryanne established Visible Changes, a chain of hair salons in Texas. Among his suggestions for success are to pursue an ambition that you really want to pursue, focus on the present, and to look inward and not outward for support and encouragement.

There were so many things I learned from reading this book. First, the fact that I READ THIS BOOK! What a huge boost to my self-esteem. It may not seem like a big deal to many, but to me, the "stupid Italian kid" who constantly beat himself up for not being able to even read, this was huge.

I also was so inspired by McCormack's success, after what many would consider a pretty huge failure. And he drew his knowledge from immigrants! Immigrants! I was an immigrant, too, and someone like him would ask someone like me for advice? That blew me away.

Then, of all businesses he chose to pursue, he opened hair salons. Now I'd known lots of amazing people who owned hair salons, but John's story really resonated with me on many levels.

Although I hadn't yet met him, John McCormack became another of my mentors. Later, I did have the opportunity to meet him and his wife and I told him how much his book and his success had meant to me. More importantly, McCormack's message is one that I have carried with me throughout my life: even with the humblest of beginnings, success is within reach.

I wasn't having as many doubts about myself as I had in the past. And I learned that I can be a good influence in the lives of others. I can be a voice of encouragement, because I now had the knowledge that we can reprogram what was programmed in our minds.

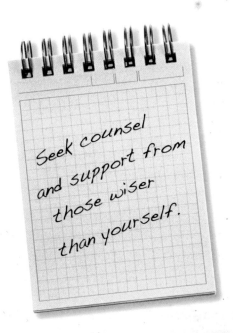

Seek counsel and support from those wiser than yourself.

19.

Going To The Light

No transformation could possibly prepare me for what would happen in 1997. I had been suffering with a deviated septum for so long. I was sick of it. I'd made the decision to have the simple surgery to correct it.

Flat on my back I stared up at the round bright cluster of lights of the operating room. I was in the spotlight. I was calm. The gentle touch of the nurse on my left pulled my eyes back to the room. She directed an encouraging smile my way as she adjusted the IV. My doctor approached on the right and placed his hand on my shoulder. He also smiled and then proceeded to check my vitals.

It was a peaceful scene. A soft purr of quiet started filling my mind. The warm blanket placed upon my torso and legs lulled me deeper into private thoughts. Out in the world, so far from this sanitary room, my life had become plentiful. My salon was doing well and the plans for my second location were drawn up and ready to roll. My family was growing. Vin and Sonny seemed to be doing okay, too. I knew I could always reconnect with these guys anytime, anywhere. It felt like I could conquer the world if I wanted to.

"Alright Giulio, are you ready?" The doctor looked down at me as he spoke through his surgical mask.

"I am. Hey doc, make me look like Al Pacino." I spoke in what seemed to be a slow monotone. For a simple elective surgery like this one for a deviated septum, that wasn't likely, but it couldn't hurt to ask, right?

His eyes squinted above his mask and a jolly, "I'll do my best," flowed to my ears. I was half floating, half sinking into that pleasant sensation of falling into a restful nap. All the detail faded from the room, my eyes closed, my hearing stopped and everything went dark. Who knew that darkness would last for 18 days?

During surgery, I had developed something called ARDS — Acute Respiratory Distress Syndrome. It is a severe injury to most or all of both lungs that has a survival rate of about 10 percent.

The doctor gathered my family in my hospital room and asked them if they believed in God. They said yes, they did. He said, "well, then now is the time to pray. Pray hard."

I remember some of my subconscious state during those 18 days. I recall sometimes being restful and peaceful, and sometimes running, fighting for my life. It was a holding time, a hiding of sorts.

In my dream world, I was sitting in an empty restaurant, at a table near a railing. The railing bordered the stairs that led down. To where, I couldn't be sure. Across from the railing on the other side of the room was a small performance stage. Near the stage was a set of double doors, the kind that swing both ways. Under the door, there was a sliver of light that shone onto the floor and into the room a bit.

There was a consciousness speaking to me. It wasn't an audible voice or words, but more of an intuitive sense. I needed to decide whether I would go down the stairs or through the double doors. For some reason, it was not immediately clear which direction I should go.

The light coming from under the doors was enticing, even welcoming. But the stairs held a certain mystery and curiosity. But as I considered my options, I realized the dark stairs caused me more fear than anything. The light under the swinging doors had a pull to it. I had to make the choice. As I pushed open the swinging doors and walked through them, I knew I was making the right decision.

"He's awake!" Someone gasped. Then I heard footsteps followed by a shriek. "He's awake you guys!" This must have been directed somewhere outside the room and into the hall.

I could feel the muscles working to open my eyes. They burned as light began to flow through. Everything was blurry, and then bit by bit, as the mixture of hushed and excited voices filled my room, I could see the detail of my family members surrounding me.

As I blinked back painful moisture and shock from the light pouring through my pupils, I could discern tear-filled eyes on the faces of every person. The last 18 days had included several near-death scares, and the ups and downs showed on the faces of those who loved me most.

My hand rose to point toward them, my mouth searched to form words and immediately the restraints of tubes in my arm and a huge tube down my throat stopped my progress.

Fear! "What's going on?" Panic rippled through

my body as I was unable to raise myself and observe my surroundings, so I grabbed on tight to my blanket and bed.

I felt more than saw a few family members rush to my side, and just as I sensed their nearness I sank back into the jet black, silent darkness.

Over the next few days I fell in and out of consciousness. Each time I woke my eyes adjusted more and more to the light, and I sought hard to find answers in the expressions on the faces of those around me. I croaked and sputtered around the obstruction in my mouth to ask, "what happened?"

I could not remember where I was. I had no idea what was going on. The longer I could remain conscious the more bits and pieces of the story my family started to relay to me. Somehow we found a way to communicate and they relived as much of the last 18 days as they could.

They explained how my body had filled with liquid and that the machines surrounding my bed and the tubes stuck in various places within my body were keeping me alive.

All I could think about was the discomfort of the situation. As I listened and tried to grasp the reality of my condition, my mind was simultaneously screaming, "please take these things out! Take them out!"

I had no way of knowing it then, but this was the beginning of a long, long road back to myself.

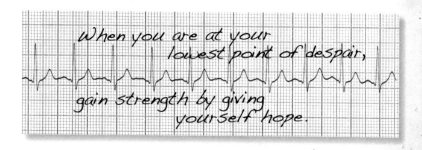

When you are at your lowest point of despair, gain strength by giving yourself hope.

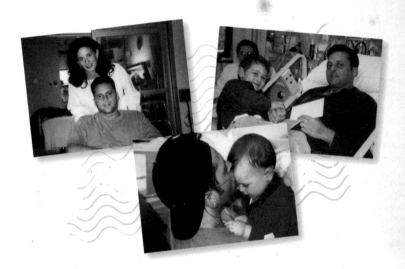

20.
Reality Check

The gentle knock pulled me from sleep. I watched my wife leaning on the door frame quietly smiling before entering the hospital room. The room that had been my recovery spot for over a month.

"Hi," she softly greeted.

"Hi," my raspy, dry voice responded.

She entered, walked over to the bed and positioned herself in the chair next to my bed. The chair she had occupied for as long as I can remember being in the bed.

I felt her take my hand. "Giulio..."

"Hmmmm?" I responded. "There's something that I have wanted to ask you and I hope you don't think this is too strange."

"Go ahead, I struggled to speak, half from the damn tube that had been down my throat and half from a slight dread of her question. "What do you want to ask?"

"Well," she said, tracing the veins on the inside of my arm. "I'm not sure I know a Vin and a Sonny. Apparently you do. You spoke of them often while coming in and out of your coma. You whisper their names and it seems as if you are talking to them while you sleep. Who are they?"

My brows raised in question as I stared up into her eyes. "Who?"

"Vin and Sonny. I'm just wondering who they are, Giulio."

My mind started to shuffle between the question and my wife's furrowed forehead. Memories of a lifetime sped through my mind. Images of my two best friends smattered through the experiences. A cool breeze floated into the hospital room, ruffling my wife's hair and mine, taking me into past expressions of our love and family. It took me into our vacations, pictures and picnics with our children. All these elements pressed in on the present, feeding a withdrawing confusion. How can my loving wife of this many years not know my lifelong buddies, Vin and Sonny?

"Babe, that's a good question. I want to tell you about my friend Vin and my friend Sonny. Right now, I can't think anymore. I need to go back to sleep. Can we talk about this later?"

"Sure Giulio," she said, brushing back my hair. She leaned in and kissed my cheek. "You sleep. I'm going to read and sit with you for a while."

"Thanks," I said, drifting off to sleep.

I'll never be sure if it came to me during a dream that day or shortly after. For days I was kind of in and out of consciousness. Thoughts, dreams, whatever seemed as much a part of reality as the fingers on my hand. Vin and Sonny appeared and disappeared. Was that real? Were they real?

In one dream I was walking down a path. Instead of trees on either side of the path, fluffy white clouds lined the way. I hadn't gone far when two men, about my size and age, approached me.

One was dressed in a button-down shirt, tie and suit. I recognized him. "Vin," I called out and increased my speed. Next to him, in a white t-shirt and jeans, was Sonny. "Hey man, how you doing?" We drew near enough. I could see the detail of their faces, and then, in a way that can only happen in dreams, their eyes captured mine and it was as if I could see inside and out of both men.

"Vin, Sonny?" I whispered, as their features melted into what seemed like mirrors reflecting slightly different versions of myself back to me. "You guys look just like me."

During the time that I was in and out of consciousness, circling on the outer edge of reality, Vin and Sonny had become even more real to me than they already had seemed at times. I had always hid my confidantes from everyone else, and especially, Laura, though I am aware that many people have friends like these.

Looking back, I realized something pretty amazing.

Everything I ever needed to succeed or fail during this life was already inside of me. My future had never been in the hands of outside forces. It had always been within my own reach. I could see that my best friend and my worst enemy were given to me to choose between and to learn from.

Give meaning to your life from inside yourself.

21.
The Voices We Listen To

While not everyone has imaginary friends the way I do, I know that everyone does have a Vin and a Sonny in one form or another. In fact, most of us have lots of Vin's and Sonny's, because they are the voices we choose to hear. For me, they are an angel on one shoulder and a devil on the other. For other people, they probably exist in different forms.

Maybe to you, Vin is your Uncle Bob — the one you look up to. He's the successful one who is always a voice of reason. He's the straight shooter who seems to know your every move before you even make it.

Vin could be your mom — the person who seems to know you the best and love you anyway. She always wants the best for you and tries to offer gentle guidance to get you there.

Maybe it was a college professor who offered you good advice during a class, or an author of a book that impressed you the right way.

Your Vin could be anyone or just a gentle stirring in your gut to do the right thing — the little white angel who sits on your shoulder. It doesn't really matter who or what Vin is in your life, the point is to realize he is there.

And to recognize Vin means we also need to recognize Sonny. We all have Sonny's in our lives, too. Sonny is the one who gets you in trouble if you listen too closely to him. It is exciting to follow his mischievous mind and yet so painful to pay the price of doing so. I loved the thrill, the natural rush I got from following Sonny's adventure and mischief.

That part of you that admires great doctors and humanitarians would respect Vin. The part of you that cheers for the rebel and empathizes with the jerk can relate to Sonny. Sonny is smart in a street kind of way. He is wildly and frantically seeking escape, I think, from boredom. This drive in him seems constant, and rather than directing his attention to more constructive outlets for his energy, the fast track, whatever goes "bling, bling," is where you'll find him.

Sonny might be your cousin Eddie, who always used to sneak pot into the family reunions. You didn't say no, but you should have.

Sonny is that kid in junior high who was always egging you on to get in fights, like he did with me!

He is the sneaky friend who shoves the pack of gum in your coat sleeve in the middle of the store, then

pushes you out the door laughing. Or maybe he is the boyfriend or girlfriend who tempts you to go just a little bit farther than you intended.

Or maybe for you, Sonny's thinking is just how you already think! Maybe that voice in the back of your head telling you to go ahead and "just try it" is always there, and your battle is constant.

So, if Vin represents the light and the positive, Sonny is the dark and negative force. They take many forms, many shapes, but there will always be others who will attempt to change your direction, some for the better, some for the worse. It's up to you to decide who to listen to.

As I look back on my life, I see that Vin and Sonny provided constant peer pressure as they shifted my thinking between right and wrong. But beyond Vin and Sonny, I have been blessed with many positive influences in my life.

Going as far back as first grade, my friend Steve DeCarlo showed me that friendship can last forever. Jean-Michel taught me that I can do anything when I believe in myself. Paul Mitchell proved that I can be somebody simply by making up my mind to do it. John McCormack boosted my confidence with his laws of success. Of course, my mother and father paved the way for me by example.

I have to single out Winn Claybaugh, a friend who is also a business partner and mentor. He invited me to have a school with him. He inspired me to write this book and to produce my motivational CDs. He was instrumental in helping me find and pursue my real passions, and, along the way, we have developed a lifelong friendship.

All in all, I can't say that I have regrets. I believe that everything that has happened or that I have done happened for a reason. Everything has formed who and what I am today. Although I've made mistakes, I'm proud of who I've become. And it's been a long, hard road to travel to get to the point where I can say that.

The most important thing to do is understand whose voice you are listening to. When you are getting a message about what you should or shouldn't do in a situation, be sure to stop, think and analyze where the thought or feeling is coming from.

Take a gut check to determine if it is a voice worth listening to or one that should be avoided at all costs. Always try to do the right thing. And never, never, never let others (friends, relatives, colleagues or voices) keep you from what you were meant to do, no matter the positive or negative forces in your life.

All conflict is manufactured inside your mind. It's never too late to let it go.

22.

Lessons Of A Life Well-Lived

The most positive influence in my life was my father. I know it must have been difficult for him sometimes, to hold his tongue and not give advice as he watched me fall on my butt while making the wrong choices. I guess that sometimes he felt that the best way for me to learn was to make my own mistakes. Throughout my life, I can now see that he knew precisely when to go in and out of advice-giving mode.

Babbo was there for me whenever I needed him. On the rare occasion that I did ask for advice, he offered his wisdom. I didn't always listen, and I didn't always take his advice, but I knew it was there if I chose to listen.

In February, 2009, as I flew to New York, I was deep in thought about my father on the entire trip. Reflections of my childhood and my life with my father zipped through my head. I was fairly sure that I was on my way to say goodbye to my father. He'd had a stroke and they were putting him on a respirator.

As I stood by his hospital bed, it was kind of a role reversal, an out-of-body experience. I couldn't help but remember when I was the one hovering near death and he was the one standing over my hospital bed in 1997.

As I studied his face, I felt like I was looking into my own future. He didn't know me, see me, or hear me, but he was still speaking to me, silently. It was like I could feel his thoughts, his reassurance that it was going to be okay. There were lessons he taught me during the days in that room. Though the only audible noise in his room was the beeping of the machines that were keeping him alive, I felt like he was telling me, "son, I have lived a good life. I am proud of what I have done and I am proud of you. I gave enough of me. I gave love to my family, my wife. I worked hard and I worked well. I did my best."

After he passed, my brother and I waited in his room for the funeral home to come and pick up his body. I knew his soul was gone from his body, but I felt him with me somehow. I felt a surge of emotion and gratitude for all he had done for me in his life. I knew he had given me a gift when he sacrificed everything he had to move his family to America, but I realized that today I had received the ultimate gift on the lessons of life from him.

At the funeral home, I was invited to give him a last haircut. I went into the embalming room where I found him on a stainless steel table waiting for me. I cut my father's hair for the last time, and as I did, I continued to think about all that I had learned from my father.

I will always admire my father for what he gave up for his family, and how he put us before his own needs. But he did even more for us by living his life by example. The way he lived is the lasting gift that will continue to bless my life, and hopefully, the lives of others as I share them.

It took my father's death to help me really see and begin to understand some of the remarkable lessons he tried to impart to me throughout my life. I guess I was a slow learner for the things that count the most. Shortly after his funeral, I began to be able to articulate what had been right in front of me all along. That's when I created this list. I hope you will find something that will resonate with you.

My Father's Lasting Lessons

Be Focused to Accept the Moment

Do not spend time in denial. This is how it is now. I had a history of overlooking anything bad or negative that I didn't want to deal with. I loved living in denial but I found that the issue rarely left as a result of my denial. It was right there waiting for me where I left it. My father taught me to deal with things as soon as they become apparent. Denial is no place to reside.

Maintain Your Body Better Than Your Car

Take care of the one and only body that you have. I, like so many others, have abused this poor body over and over again. It's incredible that I've taken better care of my car! I watched my father take good care of what God gave him. He ate right, didn't smoke and walked everywhere. Was I doing everything I could to maintain good health? No way. I needed to make some changes for my total well-being.

Take Care of Your Business

There is no point spending time in the judgment of others. My father always said that it is so tempting to tell others what they need to do when my only business should be myself. He was right. There is more than enough to judge in myself to keep me very busy without sticking my nose into the lives of others.

Live Your Legacy

The rules are simple: live life well, love your family and love your life. My father taught me that he lives on. He lives on in me. And, whether it's for the good or for the bad, I will live on in my children. How they live, how they love, how they remember me, is up to me in part. As fathers, our legacy is what we have instilled in our kids. I hope I am remembered with even half of the love and respect that my father is remembered.

Always Show Love in Your Own Way

My father understood that people are at their best when they can express themselves in their truest form. He taught me that people show love in many different ways. For example, some people show affection with gifts. Some spend time together. Some spend time apart. Some hug. Some cook wonderful meals. And, some, like my *babbo*, would show his love with a little slap on the back of the head.

And right now, what I wouldn't give for just one more slap on the back of my head!

Live your life with love.

With Much Gratitude

A wonderful benefit which comes with the writing of a book is the opportunity to indulge in the acknowledgement of the many people who have provided support and encouragement along the way.

Please allow me this time and space to offer my gratitude to the following:

My Family

My parents, Giovanni and Bianca, without them this book would not have been written. You are my hero, my role model and my master teacher. My brothers and sisters, Giuseppe, Elvira and Maria, thank you for your strength and hope. Laura, my treasured wife and loving boys, Giulio, Jr. and Stefano, I cannot thank you enough for the patience and understanding you have given me each and every day.

My aunts and uncles showed us how families support one another. Belated thanks to Anna and Frank Lotano for providing my family a home to stay and a place for us kids to wreck when we first arrived from Italy.

My Alter Egos

Sonny and Vin, I owe many important life lessons to you. Thanks for being with me through thick and thin.

My Colleagues

Paul Mitchell, I thank you for your brilliance, heart and expertise.

John Paul DeJoria enhanced my life with his

infectious attitude and can-do spirit. Thank you for opening the doorway for so many possibilities for me to succeed.

Winn Claybaugh taught me that "the more you give, the more you have." He has lived this truth throughout his life. I cannot thank you enough for your friendship and the mentoring you have given me.

Everyone involved in John Paul Mitchell Systems including Tommy Callagan, Vinny Musum, Joyce Campbell, Ellen Barbrow. Thank you for being a collection of charismatic individuals for whom creativity, courage and caring are a way of life.

The behind-the-scenes individuals I have worked with or who have worked for me, thank you for your impact in my life. You have inspired me and taught me.

Creative Collaborators

I am forever grateful to the wonderful individuals who have brought my work to life. Kudos to Merry Bateman for shaping my story into this beautiful book. Lyn Christian, thank you for patiently encouraging me to create my book. And Heather Laughter, I appreciate our talks to capture the spirit of my life. To all three of you, I cannot thank you enough in this lifetime or the next.

Authors and Gurus

John McCormack, you encouraged me and believed in me when I needed it the most. Sam Brocato, thank you for your energy, wisdom and patience. I admire who you are.

Many other authors and inspirational gurus, you know who you are and I thank you for your influence. I would need to write a whole other book to list everyone.

Bring Giulio Veglio To Your Organization Or Company

Through his company, Visionary Freak, Giulio Veglio travels the world sharing his insights to motivate and inspire others. He is fun, high energy and very engaging. It's no wonder that Giulio is highly sought after to appear at conferences, events and special programs as a keynote speaker and workshop presenter. Find out more about his presentations and availability by calling **866-998-4226** or e-mail **info@visionaryfreak.com**.

Start Listening to Giulio's Two Powerful CDs Today!

1. *Unwrapping Your Gift: Make the Most of Yourself!*

Follow along with Giulio in this two-CD set as he covers the 25 steps to success. Practical tips and suggestions that truly work for everyone.

2. *Rhythm of Success: The Power of Verbal and Non-Verbal Communication*

Giulio describes effective techniques to empower hairdressers to become more successful by developing outstanding interpersonal skills. A perfect guide to catch your rhythm of success when serving customers.

Both CDs and this book are available in bulk quantity discounts for reselling, gifts or fundraising. For more information, call **866-998-4226** or e-mail **info@visionaryfreak.com**.

To keep up with Giulio's programs and activities, visit **www.visionaryfreak.com**.